Instructor's Manual and Test Bank

to accompany

DeVito
MESSAGES:
Building Interpersonal Communication Skills

Third Edition

Prepared by
Harriet B. Harral

INSTRUCTOR'S MANUAL and TEST BANK to accompany DeVito, *Messages: Building Interpersonal Communication Skills* prepared by Harriet B. Harral.

ISBN: 0-673-97042-6

95 96 97 98 99 9 8 7 6 5 4 3 2 1

Dedicated:

To my husband, Paul --

and to our son, Huard --

and to our parents,
Joe and Gene Aubrey Briscoe
and
Edith Harral

TABLE OF CONTENTS

Chapter 12

INTERPERSONAL COMMUNICATION AND POWER

TEST BANK

True/False, Multiple Choice, Essay, and
Fill-in-the-Blank Questions for each
Chapter

TRANSPARENCY MASTERS

(Ten or more Masters for each Chapter)

INTRODUCTION TO INSTRUCTOR'S MANUAL
to Accompany *MESSAGES*

The **INSTRUCTOR'S MANUAL** is designed to help you choose the best combination of teaching methods to help your students accomplish the Learning and Skill Objectives in each chapter of **MESSAGES**. As you try various approaches suggested in the **Manual**, you will be able to assess the teaching/learning methods which are most successful for your students.

The **INSTRUCTOR'S MANUAL** provides you with a broad range of approaches. Methodologies include lecture, group discussion, practical application, self-assessment, case studies, role playing, instrumentation, and thoughts for reflection. It will allow you to choose according to the most preferred learning styles of your students.

We would encourage you to try a variety of approaches. Most of us tend to use those teaching styles with which we are most comfortable; they may or may NOT be the styles which are best suited to the learning styles of our students. Through experimentation you will be able to assess the best choices for a particular class.

Each chapter contains the following elements:

Chapter Overview
Learning Objectives
Skill Objectives
Classroom Approaches
Transparency Masters
Critical Thinking Emphasis
Skill Evaluation

CHAPTER OVERVIEW

This section summarizes the entire chapter and is built around the major headings in the text.

LEARNING OBJECTIVES

Each chapter of **MESSAGES** begins with *Learning Objectives*. These outline the major cognitive concepts dealt with in the chapter. They are repeated at the beginning of each chapter in the **INSTRUCTOR'S MANUAL** to facilitate coordinating each objective with the learning approaches illustrated in the next section. For each one we provide several classroom approaches for explanation, illustration, practice, or application.

SKILL OBJECTIVES

Related to the *Learning Objectives* are the specific *Skill Objectives* for each chapter topic. These are the heart and soul of **MESSAGES**. The main focus of the classroom approaches provided in this manual is the development of skill mastery. In addition to explaining the theories in interpersonal communication, we aim to improve the student's ability to communicate effectively in relationships with others.

CLASSROOM APPROACHES

In this section of the manual, each *Learning Objective* and *Skill Objective* will be presented with several methodological approaches from which to choose according to the needs and interests of the class being taught. Master copies for the visual aids mentioned in this section are included at the end of the manual as well as copied in the chapter.

The *Classroom Approaches* are organized according to the major topics of each chapter. The objectives related to that topic are listed, and approaches are provided to allow explanation, demonstration, and application.

The attempt throughout the classroom approaches suggested in the **INSTRUCTOR'S MANUAL** is to assist you in helping students develop skills, critical thinking, intercultural consciousness, and empowerment.

VISUAL AIDS

The **INSTRUCTOR'S MANUAL** provides *Transparency Masters* for each major topic in the chapter. These masters may be used to make overhead transparencies and/or handouts.

If you have access to a Thermofax machine, we strongly recommend your using it for overhead transparencies. While the masters could be run through a regular copier, they would be limited to black letters on clear or colored backgrounds. Colored letters on clear or contrasting backgrounds test much more effectively for impact and retention.

The *Transparency Masters* are a particularly important way of reaching visually oriented students. They will serve as reinforcement for other learners.

CRITICAL THINKING

This section selects from the text and the **ACTIVITY MANUAL** those suggestions which pertain specifically to the development of critical thinking skills. Consistent reinforcement in each chapter and related to each topic will give students an opportunity to gain mastery of this important skill.

SKILL EVALUATION

The focus of this section of each chapter in **STRATEGIES** is on the skill development of the students. The text emphasizes the need for skill mastery; the evaluation procedures in this section are designed to allow students to demonstrate that mastery.

We strongly urge that you emphasize evaluation of skills as you teach with this text. Its emphasis is on developing skill in interpersonal communication; only by focusing on that development in the evaluation process can an effective assessment be made of the student's real progress.

TEST BANK

Cognitive development may be tested with questions such as those in the Test Bank in the last section of this manual. An understanding of the theory underlying the skills being developed is essential; the test questions will allow you to focus on and reinforce that understanding.

STUDY GUIDE AND ACTIVITIES MANUAL TO ACCOMPANY MESSAGES

The *Study Guide and Activities Manual to Accompany* **MESSAGES** is an extremely helpful tool for cognitive reinforcement and skill practice. It includes a review of concepts, a study outline, vocabulary review, a sample test, diverse exercises, and readings to expand on the concepts in **MESSAGES**. The materials are organized to move the student from a fairly easy application of text material to more difficult work with concepts.

It provides additional insight and application for each of the major topics in the text. Its exercises are referenced in the *Classroom Approaches* for coordination of text material and the *Activity Manual*.

ANCILLARY MATERIALS:

In addition to the **Activity Manual** and the **Instructor's Manual** to accompany *MESSAGES*, there are two other exciting resources:

- **The Interpersonal Challenge 2: A Game to Accompany MESSAGES** by Joseph A. DeVito

   The game will assist you in helping students get to know one another in a supportive and nonjudgmental atmosphere. It also stimulates students to discuss interpersonal communication issues and experiences. You will find that it reinforces text concepts -- and is fun as well!

- **Brainstorms: How to Think More Creatively about Communication*** by Joseph A. DeVito (*** or About Anything Else**)

   This little book is a wonderful resource to expand the text's focus on critical thinking. It provides practical strategies and techniques for creativity, problem solving, and communication.

SUMMARY

We are excited about **MESSAGES,** the **ACTIVITY MANUAL,** and this **INSTRUCTOR'S MANUAL**, and we are delighted that you are using them with your class. Growth in effective interpersonal communication skills is both imperative and a cause for optimism. We hope that these books will help you motivate and educate students toward that growth.

All three of the authors of these books wish you a productive, exciting class. Let us know if we can be of assistance. We would be delighted to receive your feedback on these materials and to discuss ideas about interpersonal communication with you. Our addresses are:

Joseph A. DeVito
Department of Communication
Hunter College
695 Park Avenue
New York, NY 10021
212-772-4082

Harriet B. Harral
Harral Management Consulting Services
2102 Pembroke
Fort Worth, Texas
817-923-1120
hbharral@onramp.net

Marylin Kelly
801 Deer Ridge Road
Woodway, TX 76712
817-750-3636

Chapter 1
INTERPERSONAL COMMUNICATION

CHAPTER OVERVIEW

Interpersonal communication is defined as communication that takes place between two people who have a relationship between them. It is valuable for at least five important purposes: to learn, to relate, to influence, to play, and to help.

The major elements of interpersonal communication are the source-receiver, messages, feedback, feedforward, channel, noise, context, competence, and ethics. Interpersonal communication rests on four essential principles: 1) interpersonal communication is transactional, 2) interpersonal communication contains both content and relationship messages, 3) interpersonal communication is inevitable, and 4) interpersonal communication is irreversible and unrepeatable.

Learning Objectives

After completing this chapter, students should be able to:
1. Explain the values of studying interpersonal communication
2. Define *interpersonal communication* and its major elements
3. Explain the principles of interpersonal communication

Skill Objectives

After completing this chapter, students should improve their abilities to:
1. Interact interpersonally to serve a variety of purposes
2. Interact interpersonally with a recognition of all significant elements
3. Engage in interpersonal communication with a clear recognition of its essential principles

CLASSROOM APPROACHES

The Purposes of Interpersonal Communication (pp. 6-7)

Emphasis: Learning Objective 1
 Students will be able to explain the values of studying interpersonal communication.

Emphasis: Skill Objective 1
 Students will be able to interact interpersonally to serve a variety of purposes.

Possible Methodologies:

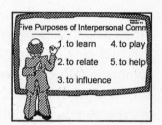

1. Lecture using the information on pp. 6-7 of **MESSAGES**. **Transparency Master 1-1** may be used as an overhead transparency to visually support the information.

2. Introduce the five purposes of interpersonal communication:

   a. Set up five separate areas of the room. Each area should have an instruction sheet explaining what students are to do in that area. Do not identify the communication purpose on the instruction sheet.

      (To Learn): Each student in this area is to teach the others something they are not likely to know.

      (To Relate): In this area, students are to visit with each other and get to know each other better.

      (To Influence): Choose a controversial topic. Students are to take opposing sides and seek to change each other's minds.

      (To Play): Share jokes and/or funny stories.

      (To Help): Share advice on how best to make a good grade in this class.

   b. As students arrive at class, divide them into five groups and assign each group to a learning area without telling them what each area represents. Ask them to spend two to three minutes following the instructions in that area.

   c. Let groups rotate through each area.

   d. When the students reassemble into the large group, tell them that the topic of discussion deals with the five purposes of interpersonal communication and that they have already experienced all five.

e.   Ask students to decide what purpose of communication each of the areas and group activities represented.

3.   The *Test Yourself: What Do You Believe About Interpersonal Communication* on pp. 5-6 of **MESSAGES** can be used as a springboard for ideas in the rest of the chapter - and the rest of the course.

The Nature of Interpersonal Communication (pp. 7-16)

Emphasis: Learning Objective 2
  Students will be able to define *interpersonal communication* and its major elements

Emphasis: Skill Objective 2
  Students will be able to interact interpersonally with a recognition of all significant elements

Possible Methodologies:

1.   Lecture using the information on pp. 7-16 of **MESSAGES**. **Transparency Master 1-2** through **1-9** may be used to make overhead transparencies to visually support the information.

2.   Explore connotations for "interpersonal communication:"
  a.   Ask students what "interpersonal communication" means to them.
  b.   List meanings on chalkboard or flip chart.
  c.   Point out both similarities and differences among the definitions.
  d.   Call the students' attention to the definition in **MESSAGES** on p. 7. Use **Transparency Master 1-2** to emphasize the significance of "relationship" in the definition.
  e.   Look up the word "interpersonal" in the dictionary. Discuss the meaning of the prefix, "inter-" (between, among, together) and of the root, "person" (a particular individual, the real self).

3.   Explore definitions of interpersonal communication:
  a.   Divide the class into groups of about five.
  b.   Ask each group to develop a definition for "interpersonal communication" and

to be prepared to explain why they feel comfortable with that definition.

    c.   After each group reports on its definition, discuss similarities and differences between the class definitions and the definition in **MESSAGES** on p. 7.

4.   Consider the significance of dyads in relationships:

    a.   Ask students to list as many significant relationships in which they are involved as they can. Remind them to consider school; home; work; religious, social and civic organizations; etc.

    b.   Within each of the general relationships listed, students should identify the one other person with whom they most frequently or meaningfully interact.

5.   Find support for the significance of dyads:

    a.   Divide the class into groups of about 5-7.

    b.   Assign each group one of the following sayings:

Two's *company; three's a crowd.*
Nine-tenths of the people were created so you would want to be with the other tenth.
"For this reason a man shall leave his father and mother, and be made one with his wife; and the two shall become one flesh." Matthew 19:5
Human *beings are social animals.* (from Baruch Spinoza)
No *one is an island, entire of itself; everyone is a piece of the continent, a part of the   main.* (from John Donne)
"Children should always play in even numbers."

    c.   Ask the groups to give examples of significant dyads which illustrate the quotation.

    d.   Each group will then share its thoughts on the quotation. Use **Transparency Master 1-3** to show the class some of the sayings being discussed.

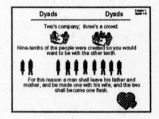

6.   Identify elements of interpersonal communication:

    a.   Divide the class into groups of seven or more.

    b.   Ask each group to prepare a short skit which will show each of the elements of interpersonal communication: source-receiver, messages, feedback, feedforward, channel, noise, context. The groups may choose to show a situation which has each of the elements in it, they may choose to personify each of the elements, or they may choose some other way to demonstrate the elements.

    c.   After each group presents its skit, ask the rest of the class to identify each of the elements of interpersonal communication demonstrated.

    d.   Use **Transparency Master 1-4** to highlight the elements of interpersonal communication.

7.   Introduce the concept of source-receiver:

    a.   Ask a student to volunteer for an exercise. Send the volunteer out of the room and ask him/her to plan something to tell the class -- a joke, an opinion about a political situation, an experience he/she has had, etc. While the volunteer plans, give the rest of the class their instructions.

    b.   Ask the class to act as receiver-senders when the volunteer speaks. Half of the class should act extremely interested and send as many positive signals as they can to the speaker. The rest of the class should act extremely uninterested and send as many negative signals as they can.

    c.   Let the volunteer speak. Afterwards, ask the volunteer how well the class did as receivers of the message. How did the volunteer feel about speaking to the class?

    d.   Discuss: who was the sender in this situation? Who was the receiver? Name some other instances when the sender-receiver combined role is very clear.

9.   Demonstrate encoding and decoding messages:

    a.   Ask students to determine the code used to construct the following number sequences. On the basis of the code, they should then predict the missing numbers. Use **Transparency Master 1-5** with the code sequences as a handout or as an overhead transparency.

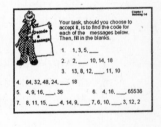

        1.   1, 3, 5, ___ (7: add 2)

        2.   2, ___, 10, 14, 18 (6: add 4)

        3.   13, 8, 12, ___, 11, 10 (9: subtract 5, add 4, subtract 3, add 2, subtract 1)

        4.   64, 32, 48, 24, ___, 18 (36: subtract half, add half, subtract half, add half, subtract half)

        5.   4, 9, 16, ___, 36 (add 5, 7, 9, 11)

6. 4, 16, __, 65536 (256: square the preceding number)
7. 8, 11, 15, __, 4, 14, 9, __, 7, 6, 10, __, 3, 12, 2 (5, 1, 13: the numbers from 1-15 are in alphabetical order)

b. Discuss the answers and codes. Why was the last one so hard? The difficulty occurs because the rationale for the code changes. Discuss real life instances in which that happens. Some suggested instances include: learning a foreign language, a significant change in a relationship, professional jargon, etc.

10. Assist the students to identify interpersonal competence.
a. Use **Transparency Master 1-6** to illustrate the goal of developing competence.
b. Ask students to plot a scale with the numbers 1 through 10 across the top of a piece of paper. (1 = low; 10 = high) Along the side they should list such contexts as School, Home, Job, Social, With Peers, With Strangers, etc. Then ask them to place an "X" on the scale beside each context to identify how interpersonally competent they feel in that context. Discuss: Why are there differences? What makes you feel competent in those contexts you rated high? What causes you to feel less competent in the contexts rated low? Encourage students to select a context for special effort during the course of the class.

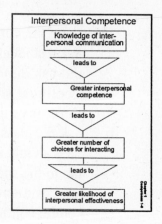

11. Demonstrate the concepts of feedback and feedforward:
a. Give each student a blindfold. After they have paper and pencil ready, ask them to blindfold themselves. Then give them the following instructions:

    Write your name and address in the upper right hand corner of the page. Then draw a map showing how to get from the location of this class to your address. Note on the map any points of reference that would be helpful.

b. Discuss the experience. How did it feel to have visual feedback limited? How accurate was their drawing? How could the situation have been improved? (Someone who could see could have given them verbal feedback as they drew, give examples of how the blind cope, etc.)
c. If you have the resources, use a soundproof room or earphones to block out aural feedback and go through a similar exercise. How does it feel to have no

aural feedback? How could you compensate for it? How do the deaf learn to speak?

d. Discuss situations in which feedback of various sorts is limited. How do you feel? How could you better compensate for limited feedback?

e. Ask students to listen for examples of feedforward and bring them to the next class meeting for discussion. Ask students to look for similarities in the kinds of situations in which they encountered feedforward (before someone tells bad news, for instance).

12. Demonstrate the variety of communication channels:
    a. Present a lecture based on the basic elements of interpersonal communication. In the lecture, use as many different channels as you can:
       Transparencies
       Slides
       Movies or videotapes
       Tape recordings
       Posters
       Models that can be felt and manipulated
       Another person
       Etc.
    b. Discuss the impact of the various channels. Did several channels help or hinder the message? What additional channels can you think of?

13. Introduce the element of noise:
    a. Play a scratchy record or show a videotape with a lot of static. Discuss reactions to physical noise.
    b. Ask students to collect examples of closed-mindedness over the next week. Discuss their examples. Use questions such as: How do you feel when someone's closed-mindedness shuts out a message you want them to hear? Can you identify any areas in which you may be closed-minded?
    c. Use **Transparency Master 1-7** to illustrate the three main types of noise.

14. Discuss the impact of context on interpersonal communication:
    a. Explain the four dimensions of context (physical, cultural, social-psychological,

and temporal). Use **Transparency Master 1-8** for support.

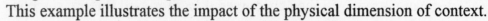

b. Give an example of a statement, the meaning of which changes as the context changes:
"She ran over him" is a statement which means one thing in a hospital, and quite another on a tennis court.
This example illustrates the impact of the physical dimension of context.

c. Ask students to get in groups of 5-6 and develop three similar examples to share with the class. Each example should relate to a different dimension of context.

15. Use *Activity 1: Communication Models* on p. 8 of the **ACTIVITY MANUAL** to help students conceptualize the elements of interpersonal communication.

16. Examine the role of ethics in the decisions we make about communication.

a. Ask students to compete *Skill Building Exercise 1.1: Ethics in Interpersonal Communication* in **MESSAGES**, p. 13-14. Conduct a discussion of ethical principles used to make the decisions in the situations listed.

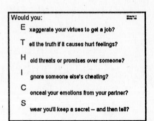

b. Use **Transparency 1 - 9** to pose questions to the class about ethical dilemmas. Ask: How often are they faced with ethically difficult choices?

17. *Activity 2: Learning from Others* on p. 9 of the **ACTIVITY MANUAL** provides an opportunity for students to apply concepts from the models of communication. In addition, ask students to identify principles of ethical behavior in the three people they identify as effective communicators.

Principles of Interpersonal Communication (pp. 17-23)

Emphasis: Learning Objective 3
Students will be able to explain the principles of interpersonal communication.

Emphasis: Skill Objective 3:
Students will be able to engage in interpersonal communication with a clear recognition of its essential principles.

Possible Methodologies:

1. Lecture using the information on pp. 17-23. **Transparency Master 1-10** may be used to visually support the information.

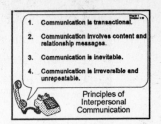

2. Explain the principle that communication is transactional.
    a. Elaborate on the text information with further explanation of different models of communication: one-way, two-way, technical vs. interpersonal, etc. Discuss how one's assumptions about how communication works influence how one goes about communicating.

    b. Ask the class to respond to the following questions: (write their responses on the chalkboard or flip chart)
    What does it mean to say that communication has no clear-cut beginning or ending?
    Give an example which illustrates that idea.
    How might knowing this concept influence the way you go about communicating?

3. Demonstrate the principle that we communicate both content and relationship messages:
    a. Arrive at class in an obviously angry mood. Conduct class normally, but let your anger show. Be sarcastic and caustic. Insist on the class following some rather ridiculous instructions even if they protest. (For instance, insist on a particular complicated format the class must use for their notes. Say that you are going to take up their notebooks and grade them.)
    b. After about 15 minutes of such behavior, stop and ask the class:
    How do I feel today?
    How do I feel about you today?
    Identify the content of my message today.
    What does my insistence on following my instructions tell you about the way I feel about our relationship? Where is the power? authority?

    c. Discuss the need to look for relationship messages within messages that seem strictly content. Use **Transparency Master 1-11** to illustrate the idea.
    d. Discuss the difference between content messages and

relationship messages. Ask the class to see if they can think of a message that is strictly content and no relationship. See if they can think of one that is strictly relationship and no content.

e. Use *Skill-Building Exercise 1.3, Predicting Relational Messages* on pp. 21-22 of **MESSAGES** to give students an opportunity to practice assessing relational messages and to examine their own assumptions.

6. Demonstrate the inevitability of communication.
   a. Ask for five volunteers. Seat them at the front of the room. Include yourself as one of the volunteers.
   b. Ask the class to answer the following questions about each of the volunteers.
      I. *Did they come from an urban area or a rural one?*
      ii. *Do they come from a large family or a small one?*
      iii. *Do they make mostly A's, B's, or C's?*
      iv. *Do they live on-campus or off?*
      v. *Are they Protestant, Catholic, non-denominational, unaffiliated?*
      vi. *Are they Democrat or Republican?*
      vii. *Are they married or single?*
      viii. *What are they majoring in?*
      ix. *Do they have children?*
      x. *Do they work? If so, what sort of job?*
   c. Ask for a show of hands on the responses to the questions. Discuss how people decided on their answers. How did each of the volunteers "communicate" to the class? How much of what was communicated was likely to be a conscious message as opposed to an inadvertent one? Point out that the volunteers were simply sitting at the front of the room. They were not trying to send messages, and yet they did so.

7. Demonstrate the principle that we cannot reverse communication:
   a. Apply the principle to the area of libel laws. How do such laws illustrate the principle that communication cannot be reversed?
   b. Discuss the effectiveness of a judge's injunction to a jury to ignore something they have just heard.
   c. Ask students to identify a time they wished they could reverse communication. What happened? Did they try to change the impact of the communication? Were they successful or not?

Try NOT to think of a pink rhinoceros!

d. Use **Transparency 1-12** to illustrate that once something is said, it is hard to ignore it.

8. *Activity 3: I Wish I Had Said...* on p. 11 of the **ACTIVITY MANUAL** gives students an opportunity to analyze an experience of their own in which they wish communication could be reversible.

9. *Skill-Building Exercise 1.2: Explaining Interpersonal Difficulties* in **MESSAGES**, pp. 17-18, provides an excellent opportunity to review the principles of communication.

10. In order to help students think of ways to improve communication, assign them to read *Activity 5: Barriers to Communication* on p. 13 of the **ACTIVITY MANUAL**.

Critical Thinking Skills

Possible Methodologies:

1. Review the *Critical Thinking and Interpersonal Communication Sidebar* on p. 5 of **MESSAGES**. Note that one characteristic of critical thinking mentioned in *Critical Thinking Sidebar: Why? What?* on p. 7 is the ability to raise powerful questions. Ask students to be prepared with at least one question per section of the chapter.

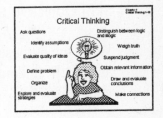

2. *Critical Thinking Sidebar: The Skills of Critical Thinking* on p. 8 of **MESSAGES** lists 12 skills. At the end of the chapter, ask students which ones they put into play during their study of Chapter 1. Were any of the skills particularly difficult? Use **Transparency Master 1-13**.

3. Ask the class to give you examples of how they each decided on a major, or how they decided to attend your school.
    a. List the ideas on the board or a flip chart.
    b. Ask the students to identify examples of critical thinking skills in the ideas listed.

4.	Explore the STEP process described in *Critical Thinking Sidebar: Learning Skills* on p. 17 of **MESSAGES**. Use **Transparency Master 1-14** for visual support.
   a.	Assign each student to develop a plan to teach a skill to the class.
   b.	The plan must include:
      I.	identification of a specific skill
      ii.	explanation of relevant theory
      iii.	meaningful examples
      iv.	practice
   c.	Ask for volunteers to present their learning plan to the class.
   d.	Ask the class to respond to each plan. Would the STEP process presented be helpful?

3.	Apply the STEP process to an overview of the chapters in the text.
   a.	Briefly point out specific skills to be learned.
   b.	Give students a few minutes to glance through the text to see how theory, examples and opportunities for practice are included in each chapter.

4.	Use *Activity 6: Messages and Me* on p. 19 of the **ACTIVITY MANUAL** to encourage students to explore ideas in this chapter critically by keeping a communication journal.

SKILL EVALUATION

I.	Skill Objective 1: Interact interpersonally to serve a variety of purposes

Write the purposes for interpersonal communication on separate pieces of paper and ask each student to draw one when his/her turn comes. The student must then choose another student and demonstrate the purpose drawn.

II.	Skill Objective 2: Interact interpersonally with a recognition of all significant elements

Provide a script from a play with a scene between two characters. Ask two students to work together to act out the scene. They should provide script notes indicating the spots which best illustrate each of the elements of interpersonal communication and then act them out in ways which make clear to the audience which element is being demonstrated.

III. Skill Objective 3: Apply the principles of communication to gain greater understanding of interpersonal interactions

A. Place students in pairs. Each pair of students should plan an interaction which will allow them to demonstrate all four principles of interpersonal effectiveness. They must then present their interaction to the rest of the class which will be assigned to identify each of the qualities as they are demonstrated.

B. Ask student to identify content and relationship messages in selected communication situations. A good source for examples of content and relationship messages is <u>Are You Sure You Love Me?</u> by Lois Wyse (The World Publishing Company, 1969). Particularly good are "Anniversary Song," "Nobody Listens to Me," "7:15 p.m.," and "10 p.m."

C. Use the situations in *Skill-Building Exercise 1.2: Explaining Interpersonal Difficulties* on p. 17 of **MESSAGES** . Ask students to choose a principle to apply to one or more of the situations and then to act or write out what they expect to happen.

Chapter One: Interpersonal Communication

Chapter 2
THE SELF

CHAPTER OVERVIEW

This chapter explores the self in interpersonal communication. One's self concept develops from at least three sources:

1. The image of you that others have
2. The comparisons you make between yourself and others
3. The way you interpret your own thoughts and behaviors

Learning about ourselves involves learning about four selves:

1. The open self: what we and others know about us
2. The blind self: what others know but we do not know
3. The hidden self: what we know but keep hidden from others
4. The unknown self: what neither we nor others know

We may increase our self awareness by asking ourselves about ourselves, listening to others, actively seeking information about ourselves, seeing ourselves from different perspectives, and enlarging our open selves.

In self-disclosure we reveal new information about ourselves to someone. It involves at least one other individual and is usually reciprocal. It allows us to gain self knowledge, increase communication effectiveness, enhance the meaningfulness of interpersonal relationships, and promote physical health. Self disclosure has dangers as well as benefits. There are several guidelines for effective self disclosure. Consider the following:

1. What is my motive for self-disclosing?
2. Is this self-disclosure appropriate to the communication situation?
3. Is the other person also disclosing?
4. Will this self-disclosure impose any possible burdens?

We have a responsibility to respond appropriately when someone self-discloses to us. Guidelines in that situation include:

1. Practice effective and active listening.
2. Support the discloser.
3. Keep the disclosures confidential.

"Communication apprehension" refers to a feeling of fear or anxiety about a situation in which one must communicate. Such apprehension can be managed through use of the following strategies:

1. Acquire communication skills and experience.
2. Focus on success.

---

3.   Reduce unpredictability.
4.   Become familiar with the situation.

Learning Objectives

After completing this chapter, students should be able to:
1. Define *self-concept* and explain how it develops
2. Explain the Johari window and define the open, blind, hidden, and unknown selves
3. Explain the suggestions for increasing self-awareness
4. Define *self-disclosure* and explain the potential rewards and dangers
5. Identify the guidelines for (a) making self-disclosures and (b) responding to the disclosures of others
6. Define *communication apprehension*, its causes, and suggested ways of managing apprehension

Skill Objectives

After completing this chapter, students should improve their abilities to:
1. Analyze their own self-concept, its sources and present state
2. Become more aware of their own communications, especially their degree of openness
3. Increase their own self awareness
4. Regulate their self-disclosures on the basis of topic, receiver, purpose, and more
5. Self-disclose and respond to the disclosures of others appropriately
6. Manage their fear of communicating
7. Communicate confidence in a variety of communication settings

---

CLASSROOM APPROACHES

Self-Concept (pp. 28-29)

Emphasis: Learning Objective 1
    Students will be able to define *self-concept* and explain how it develops.

Emphasis: Skill Objective 1

Students will improve their ability to analyze their own self-concept, its sources and present state.

Possible Methodologies:

1.   Lecture using the information in **MESSAGES**, pp. 28-29.   Use **Transparency Master 2-1** for an introduction.

2.   Help students define their own self-concepts:
      a.   Ask students to write the words, "I am a person who--" at the top of a sheet of paper. They should then finish that sentence with ten different phrases. The phrases should identify significant information -- those things which are most important. (e.g., I am a person who: really wants to become an attorney, has two children, likes to hunt, has four brothers, believes in the Democratic party, etc.)
      b.   Place the students in dyads and ask them to introduce themselves to each other using the information on their sheets of paper.
      c.   Then say that they may have only five of the items on their lists. Which five would they eliminate? Ask the dyads to discuss how this feels.
      d.   Now tell the students to trim their lists to the one most significant item on it. Ask them to discuss why they chose the item they kept.

3.   Help students contrast their own self-images with the images others have of them.
      a.   Ask students to develop artwork showing a logo for themselves. They could also decide on a personalized license plate or a bumper sticker proclaiming who they are.
      b.   After students have developed their logo, license plate, or bumper sticker, post them on the walls around the room. Number each of them.
      c.   Give the students a list of all the members of the class. Ask them to look at the artwork and decide which piece of art belongs to which classmate. Put the number of the artwork beside the name of each student.
      d.   Let students reveal their ownership and ask how many guessed correctly. Let each student get a sampling of which other artworks were identified as theirs.

---

e.   Either discuss or let students write about their reactions to this exercise. Were their self-concepts confirmed by the class guesses? Were they surprised by the choices others made for them? What did they learn about others' images for them?

f.   Other alternatives include: ask someone else to draw a logo representing you, or take your logo to friends and family and ask if they would change it in some way. In either case, ask why.

4.   Discuss social comparisons by asking students to list all the ways they can think of in which they are officially compared with others. (e.g., GPA, SAT scores, class standings, rush parties, clothes sizes, military rank, etc.) How significant are these comparisons to them? Which ones are really important?

5.   *Activity 2: The Three Selves* on p. 33 of the **ACTIVITY MANUAL** can be used to help students look at themselves in several different ways and then help them interpret the results of their examination.

Self-Awareness: Your Four Selves (pp. 30-32)

Emphasis: Learning Objective 2
      Students will be able to explain the Johari window and define the open, blind, hidden, and unknown selves.

Emphasis: Skill Objective 2
      Students will improve their ability to become more aware of their own communications, especially their degree of openness.

Possible Methodologies:

1.   Lecture using the information in **MESSAGES** on pp. 30-32. **Transparency Master 2-2** may be used to visually support the information.

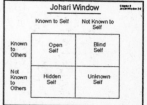

2.   As you explain each of the quadrants in the Johari Window, ask students to give appropriate examples for it. List them in the quadrant, thereby making it the largest of the four. Demonstrate how it impacts the other quadrants as it gets larger. Continue to adjust the sizes of the Johari Window as you collect examples from the class.

3.   Provide students with a large drawing of the Johari Window. Assign them to ask twelve other people to list something about the student in each of the quadrants. The student should then write a brief reaction paper.

4.   Use *Activity 1: Johari Window* on p. 32 of the **ACTIVITY MANUAL** to increase familiarity with the four selves.

Increasing Self-Awareness (pp. 32-38)

Emphasis: Learning Objective 3
       Students will be able to explain the suggestions for increasing self-awareness.

Emphasis: Skill Objective 3
       Students will increase their own self awareness.

Possible Methodologies:
1.   Lecture using information on pp. 32-38 of **MESSAGES**. Use **Transparency Master 2-3** to visually support the information.

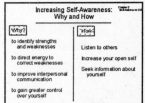

2.   Use *Skill-Building Exercise 2.1, Dialoguing with Yourself*, on pp. 34-35 of the text. Suggest that students save these worksheets so that they can review them periodically and be reminded of their self-improvement goals. They should continue the dialogue with themselves since they are constantly changing.

3.   Encourage students to listen to others and to actively seek out information about themselves by assigning them to keep a journal for three days about what people say or imply about them. On the third day, ask students to share information they feel comfortable with. Under what circumstances did they receive the information? How do they feel about it?

4.   Use John Malloy's research methodology in **Dress for Success** as a model for an assignment. Place students in pairs and send them to a mall. One student should ask passers-by to answer some questions about the other student based on nothing but the appearance of the student. Questions might include:
       How intelligent is this student?
       How old is the student?

> *How long has the student lived in our town?*
> *Would you like to get to know this student?*
> *etc.*

Then the students should switch questioner and subject. Report on experiences in class.

5. Help all members of the class to enlarge their open selves by asking them to think of one thing about themselves that nobody in the class knows and then take turns telling about it.

6. Standardized personality-type instruments are a good way to help people expand their understanding of themselves. The **Myers-Briggs Type Indicator** (Center for Applications of Psychological Type, Inc., 2720 N.W. 6th Street, Gainesville, FL 32609) and the **Strength Deployment Inventory** (Personal Strengths Publishing, Inc., P.O. Box 397, Pacific Palisades, CA 90272) are both excellent and well validated. Ask a trained facilitator to administer the instrument and then give feedback to the class as a group as well as to the individuals in the class. These may allow students to fill in some information in their blind or unknown quadrants. Many college and university counseling offices have these tests available.

Self Disclosure (pp. 38-48)

Emphasis: Learning Objectives 4 and 5
Students will be able to:
4. Define *self-disclosure* and explain the potential rewards and potential dangers.
5. Identify the guidelines for (a) making self-disclosures and (b) responding to the disclosures of others.

Emphasis: Skill Objective 4
Students will improve their ability to self-disclose and respond to the disclosures of others appropriately.

Possible Methodologies:

1. Lecture using the information on pp. 38-48. Use **Transparency Masters 2-4 through 2-9** for visual support.

2.   Use the *Self Test, How Willing to Self-Disclose Are You?*, on pp. 38-39 of **MESSAGES**. Critical Thinking questions may be addressed in small groups or with the entire class. Use **Transparency Master 2-4** to discuss the factors involved in their willingness to self-disclose.

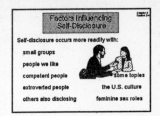

3.   Divide the class into one group of men and one group of women. Do a partial replication of research done by Lawrence Rosenfeld in 1979. Use a modified nominal group procedure as follows:

   a.   Each individual lists the three to five main reasons he or she avoids self-disclosure.
   b.   Within the group of men, and within the group of women, ask the students to share their reasons one at a time. As a student gives a reason, have a recorder list it on a flip chart. Then the second student gives a reason which is listed, and so forth until all students have given all their reasons. There is no need to list duplicate reasons. During the listing of reasons, there is to be no discussion other than clarification.
   c.   With the women looking at their list and the men looking at theirs, ask each individual to choose the three most accurate reasons for themselves from the entire list. Prioritize the three by giving the most preferred reason a "3", the next most preferred a "2", and the least preferred a "1". Write each one with its rank on a separate card. When the men and the women have completed their individual rankings, collect all the cards in each group.
   d.   Add the ranks for each item listed. The three items with the highest total are the three most preferred reasons for the men and the three most preferred reasons for the women. Write these on the flip charts at the front.

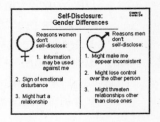

   e.   Compare the responses of the men and the women with the kinds of responses Rosenfeld obtained as listed on **Transparency Master 2-5**.

4.   Set up a debate on the rewards vs. the dangers of self-disclosure. Use **Transparency Masters 2-6 and 2-7**. Divide the class into groups of four. Ask half of the groups to develop a three minute argument in favor of self-disclosure, and ask half of the groups to develop a three-minute argument stressing the dangers. Each group should designate a speaker. Alternate speakers pro and con.

At the conclusion of the speeches, take a vote of the class: do they feel the advantages outweigh the dangers of self-disclosure, or vice versa?

5.   Use *Activity 4: How to Help Your Partner Open Up* on p. 42 of the **ACTIVITY MANUAL**. Ask students for examples of communication stoppers.

6.   Use the *Critical Thinking Sidebar: Relationship Assertions* on p. 41 and *Critical Thinking Sidebar: Causal Assertions* on p. 42 of **MESSAGES** to examine the claims relating self-disclosure and relationship duration as well as self-disclosure and physiological health. Ask the students to examine their own experiences. What conclusions might they draw in these two areas?

7.   After students read *The Art of Facilitating Self-Disclosure* on pp. 43-45 of **MESSAGES**, ask them to reflect on situations they have encountered in which self-disclosure was effectively shut off. They might write a script of their own, or take turns having groups of students act out their examples.

8.   *Skill-Building Exercise 2.2:   To Disclose or Not to Disclose?* on pp. 47-48 of **MESSAGES** will help students practice the guidelines for self-disclosure. Use **Transparency Master 2-8** for reference during the discussion. Ask the students to apply the guidelines to each of the situations listed, and then to vote on whether self-disclosure is appropriate or not.

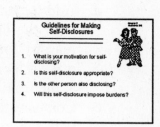

9.   Provide examples of self-disclosure from such books as **The Chamber** by John Grisham (New York: Doubleday, 1994), **The Alienist** by Caleb Carr (New York: Bantam Books, 1995), or **The Prince of Tides** by Pat Conroy (New York: Bantam Books, 1986), Have students find examples of the guidelines for responding to self-disclosures. Use **Transparency Master 2-9**.

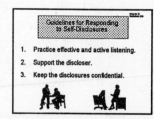

Apprehension (pp. 48-51)

Emphasis: Learning Objective 6
>Students will be able to define *communication apprehension*, its causes, and suggested ways of managing apprehension.

Emphasis: Skill Objectives 5 and 6
>Students will improve their ability to:
>5. Manage their fear of communicating
>6. Communicate confidence in a variety of communication settings

Possible Methodologies:
1. Lecture using information on pp. 48-51. Use **Transparency Masters 2-10** and **2-11** for support.

2. Give students the *Test, "How Apprehensive Are You?"* on pp. 48-49 in **MESSAGES**. Reassure them that apprehension is very common and that it can be managed. Use **Transparency Master 2-10.**

Communication Apprehensi

"Communication apprehension is probably the most common handicap suffered by people in contemporary American society."

McCroskey & Wheeless, 1976

3. Ask for six volunteers to do some role-playing. Assign them in dyads to one of the situations below. They are to act out the situations, attempting to demonstrate confidence throughout. While they do that, the class should be watching for behaviors which communicate confidence.
   a. A job interview: You are applying for a job in your field of expertise. You have the exact qualifications the job calls for, and in addition, you have worked as an intern with the same company and have rave references from your supervisor and the executive vice president. Your interviewer is Dr. Romero, manager of the department.

   b. You want to date Pat and you know that Pat would have asked you out except for extreme shyness. You've decided to ask Pat for a date. Show the interaction between yourself and Pat.

   c. You are the captain of the school's soccer team which has just won a national championship and will be traveling for international competition. You scored the winning goal and are being besieged by reporters asking for your reactions. (The entire class may play the part of the reporters.)

---

5.   Conduct deep breathing exercises with the class to illustrate greater vocal control (a way to stop a trembling voice). Also do exercises with head, arms and upper torso to relax muscles and manage symptoms of apprehension such as a strained voice, shaking hands, and breathlessness.

6.   *Activity 3: Overcoming Shyness: A Contract* on p. 39 of the **ACTIVITY MANUAL** leads students to develop a contract of behaviors to lessen communication apprehension.

7.   Use **Transparency Master 2-11** to reinforce the information on managing apprehension. Ask for an example of each suggestion.

Critical Thinking

Possible Methodologies:
1.   Using *Critical Thinking Sidebar: Transferring Skills* on p. 33 of **MESSAGES**, ask students to select one specific skill in this chapter to apply in at least three different situations. Students may report their experiences in a written paper, in classroom discussion, or through skits.

2.   Assign students to read *Self Confidence: The Art of Being You* on pp. 35-38 of **MESSAGES**. Ask students to draw or write a depiction on themselves first showing their self image based on their own experiences, and second showing their self image based on what they think people think of them. Post pictures (or paragraphs) on the wall without names and ask the class to look at each and then write down who they think is being depicted. Let students see the answers and then reveal which drawings are theirs.

        A second approach to dealing with this article is as follows: assign students to groups of four; ask each person in each group to write or draw their impression of each of the other students. Then write or draw their own self image. Compare impressions. Discuss how consistent or inconsistent the self images where with the images of others.

3.   Ask students to identify a decision they are in the process of making. They should analyze the decision in light of *Critical Thinking Sidebar: Critical Thinking Attitudes* on p. 47 of **MESSAGES**.

4. Place students in random groups of three or four. Review the chapter by having them discuss the questions in *Critical Thinking Sidebar: Discovery* on p. 51 of **MESSAGES**.

5. *Activity 5: Messages and Me* on p. 46 of the **ACTIVITY MANUAL** to encourage students to write in their journals about their insights regarding their self concept after studying this chapter.

SKILL EVALUATION

I. Skill Objective 1: Analyze your own self concept, its sources and present state

Ask students to write three paragraphs, one describing their self concept in elementary school, one for high school, and one for college. After each paragraph, students should identify a source for that description: an image from others, a comparison of themselves with others, and/or an interpretation/evaluation of their own behaviors.

II. Skill Objective 2: Become more aware of your own communications, especially your degree of openness

Place students in dyads when you begin Chapter 2. Ask them to share their self-concepts with each other. Over the course of the rest of the semester, they should meet regularly in an effort to apply class concepts. At the end of the semester, ask students to assess their own openness with their partner. Then ask the partners to assess each other's openness.

III. Skill Objective 3: Increase your own self-awareness

Use pp. 34-35, *Skill-Building Exercise 2.1: Dialoguing with Yourself*, of **MESSAGES**. Have students identify two or three Self-Improvement Goals to concentrate on over a given period of time. At the end of that time, ask them to assess whether the goals listed have been achieved. If not, why? What might they do next in an effort to make progress on their goals?

IV.   Skill Objective 4: Self-disclose and respond to the self-disclosures of others appropriately

    A. Divide class into groups of three. The groups are to write three case studies of situations involving self-disclosure. All six guidelines for making self-disclosures and the three guidelines for responding to disclosures should be illustrated in the case studies, but they may be positive or negative illustrations.   Give group grades for the case studies.

       Use the case studies written by the groups as a part of the final test. Choose several of the best ones and ask students individually to use the guidelines to assess the appropriateness of the self-disclosure.

    B. Use *Skill-Building Exercise 2.2: To Disclose or Not to Disclose?* on pp. 47-48 of **MESSAGES** as an evaluation instrument. Ask students to list reasons they would or would not self-disclose, including topic, receiver, purpose, and more.

V.   Skill Objective 5: Manage fear of communicating.

       Refer back to the self test, *How Apprehensive Are You?* on pp. 48-49 of **MESSAGES**. Assign students a task relating to a behavior for which they had the highest apprehension. They should use the four suggestions for managing apprehension and write an analysis of how successful they were.

VI.   Skill Objective 6: Communicate confidence in a variety of communication settings.

       Set individual or small group appointments with each student as part of the final evaluation. Use this opportunity to administer part of the evaluation orally. During the meeting, assess the student's ability to display confidence in a stressful situation.

Chapter 3
PERCEPTION IN INTERPERSONAL COMMUNICATION

CHAPTER OVERVIEW

Each person interprets the world differently. This chapter explores interpersonal or people perception, the way people sense, organize, and interpret-evaluate information about people.

Five processes influence perception: first impressions, implicit personality theories, self-fulfilling prophecies, stereotyping, and attribution. These five processes can also set up specific barriers to communication.

Successful interpersonal communication depends largely on the accuracy of interpersonal perception. Two steps are involved in an effort toward perception checking:

Describe (tentatively) what you think is happening.

Ask the other person for confirmation.

Learning Objectives

After completing this chapter, students should be able to:
1. Explain what perception is and how it works
2. Define the five processes that influence perception: primacy and recency, the self-fulfilling prophecy, implicit personality theory, stereotyping, and attribution
3. Explain the barriers to accurate perception that each of these processes can set up
4. Identify the strategies for increasing accuracy in interpersonal perception

Skill Objectives

After completing this chapter, students should be able to:
1. Perceive others with the recognition that they are a major part of their own perceptions

---

> 2. Perceive others while avoiding such common barriers as seeing what one wants or expects to see, pygmalion effects, fulfilling one's own predictions seeing an individual primarily as a member of a group, mind reading, and the self-serving bias.
> 3. Use the strategies for increasing accuracy in interpersonal perception.

CLASSROOM APPROACHES

Interpersonal Perception (pp. 58-62)

Emphasis: Learning Objective 1
Students will be able to explain what perception is and how it works.

Emphasis: Skill Objective 1
Students should be able to perceive others with the recognition that they are a major part of their own perceptions.

Possible Methodologies:

1. Set an atmosphere for thinking about varying perceptions by having music playing as students arrive for class. Suggested songs are "*World Apart*" as sung in the Broadway musical, **Big River**, and "*Let's Call the Whole Thing Off*" from **Annie Get Your Gun**. Classical, new age, or country western all could be used to set a different context.

2. Introduce the idea that we each see the world differently:
   a. Use optical illusions to illustrate various perceptions. An excellent resource for optical illusions is **Optricks** by Melinda Wentzell and D. K. Holland (San Francisco: Troubadour Press, 1973).
   b. As you show each illusion, ask students what they see. Collect responses.
   c. Point out the variety of answers. Ask students if they can see the things other students saw. Sometimes they will be able to see a new image when it is simply called to their attention. In other cases, they will not be able to see anything but their first impression. Discuss how strong first impressions are.
   d. Take additional steps to try to help students take another person's perception. Choose a student with a perception not shared by many others in the class. Ask

the student to describe what he/she sees; ask the class how many additional students now see the image. Then ask the student to trace the perception on the projected image. Again ask the class how many additional students see the image. Discuss the difficulty of taking another's perspective.

3. Lecture using the information on pp. 58-62 of **MESSAGES**. **Transparency Masters 3-1** and **3-2** may be used to visually support the information.

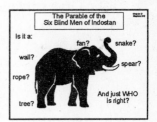

4. Introduce Stage One of Perception (Sensing):
   a. Our senses are limited physiologically:
      I. Read "The Parable of the Blind Men and the Elephant" on p. 59 of **MESSAGES**. Use **Transparency Master 3-2**.
      ii. Consider physical impairments we might experience in sight, hearing, smell, taste and touch. How do those impairments impact communication?
      iii. Ask students to list physical limitations we experience daily. Write them on a flip chart or chalk board. Suggestions:
         a. Telephone
         b. Separation by distance
         c. Cultural norms limiting touch and smell
         d. Vantage point
   b. Our senses are limited psychologically.
      I. We see what we are *interested* in. If you are driving through town and you are hungry, what are you likely to see? If you drive through the same town when you are in the market for a car, what do you see?
      ii. We see what we have **learned** to see. For example, if a police officer, a doctor and a mechanic all see the same accident, they are likely to focus on different aspects of it:
         the officer will see who was at fault
         the doctor will see injuries to the people
         the mechanic will see injuries to the cars
      iii. Use *Critical Thinking Sidebar: Your Role in Perception* on p. 59 of **MESSAGES** to discuss how biases impact what and how we perceive others.

3. Introduce Stage Two (Organizing)
   a. Use the none-dot puzzle to demonstrate the idea that we organize perceptual stimuli. This exercise is found in **Human Communication Handbook** by Brent D. Rubin and Richard W. Budd (Rochelle Park, N.J.: Hayden Book Co., Inc., 1975, p. 40.)
      I. Draw the nine dot figure on the board:

      . . .

      . . .

      . . .

      ii. Give students the following instructions:
          a. Connect all nine dots with four straight lines.
          b. You may not retrace a line.
          c. You may not lift your pen or pencil from the time you begin until you finish.
          d. You may cross lines.
      iii. After time for all students to try to solve the problem, ask if any have been successful. If so, have them demonstrate the correct answer:

      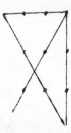

      iv. Discuss reasons for the difficulty of the exercise:
          a. How did students "organize" the dots? (Most think of them as a square or a box.)
          b. What rules did students set for themselves? (Most think they must stay within the boundaries of the square -- that they cannot go outside the "lines.")
      v. Ask students for examples of having conceptualized (organized) information incorrectly. What problems resulted?
      vi. Ask students for examples of having conceptualized (organized) information in a particularly useful way (e.g., scientific method, outlines, re-ordering of priorities, etc.). What benefits resulted?

b. Demonstrate how we organize information on the basis of a pattern which is meaningful to us by using an exercise found in Ruben and Budd, **Human Communication Handbook**, p. 45.

   I.   Ask the class to add numbers out loud as you write them on the chalkboard.

   ii. One at a time, put the following list of numbers on the board. Pause after each one for the class to call out the total:

$$
\begin{array}{r}
1000 \\
1000 \\
20 \\
1000 \\
40 \\
1000 \\
30 \\
1000 \\
\underline{10} \\
\end{array}
$$

   iii. At this point, most students will call out "6000" even though the accurate total is 5100. Discuss factors leading to the inaccurate total.

   a. What organizing principle were students using? (jumping by 1000's, dealing with large increments, etc.)

   b. Ask students to name some situations when they were operating on inaccurate expectations. What happened?

4. Introduce Stage Three (Interpreting-Evaluating)

a. Demonstrate varying interpretations of sense data by collecting a variety of items such as cotton balls, an orange peel, blades of grass, roofing shingles, shotgun shells, paint pellets, gumballs, letter opener, Slime, baking powder mixed with water, etc. Blindfold students and ask them to interpret the items. How well can they determine what each item is?

b. Use **Transparency Master 3-3** to discuss emotional reactions. You could also make a series of slides for students to evaluate. These might include such pictures as a locally controversial politician, national and international figures, music groups, various animals, obvious Republican groups, obvious Democratic groups, an abortion clinic, the KKK, a

Save the Whales group, etc. The slides should be designed to elicit widely different emotional reactions.

      I.   Show each slide (or use a reveal technique on the overhead transparency) and ask all students who assess that picture positively to gather on one side of the room; all those who evaluate it negatively should stand on the other side of the room.

      ii.   Discuss why a single stimuli can elicit very different interpretations and evaluations.

    d.   Use *Activity 3: Can you Imagine Why They Said Those Things?!* on p. 58 of the **ACTIVITY MANUAL** to illustrate different interpretations of the same statement.

    e.   *Activity 5: When Did I Become the Mother and the Mother Become the Child?* on p. 65 of the **ACTIVITY MANUAL** deals with interpretations-evaluations and how they change as we mature.

Interpersonal Perception Principles (pp. 62-72)

Emphasis: Learning Objectives 2 and 3
Students will be able to:
2. Define the processes that influence perception: *primacy and recency, the self-fulfilling prophecy, implicit personality theory, stereotyping, and attribution*
3. Explain the barriers to accurate perception that each of these processes can set up

Emphasis: Skill Objective 2
Students should be able to perceive others while avoiding such common barriers as seeing what you want or expect to see, pygmalion effects, fulfilling their own predictions, seeing an individual primarily as a member of a group, mind reading, and the self-serving bias.

Possible Methodologies:
1. Lecture using the information on pp. 62-72. **Transparency Masters 3-4 through 3-7** may be used to visually support the information.

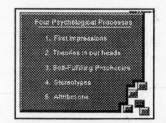

2.   Use the *Test Yourself, How Accurate Are You at People Perception?*, on pp. 62-63 in **MESSAGES** to introduce concepts in the chapter.

3.   Explore the impact of first impressions with the following assignment:
   a.   Ask students to write down their first impressions of 10 strangers they encounter on campus or in town. What about each individual led to the impression described?
   b.   Ask students to think of three of their best friends. What were their first impressions of each of the friends? Have the first impressions changed or been reinforced? Why?
   c.   Remind students of the saying, "You never have a second chance to make a first impression." Use **Transparency Master 3-5**.

You never have
a second chance
to make a
first impression.

4.   Utilize *Activity 6: Messages and Me -- The Warm-Cold Variable in First Impressions of Persons* on p. 68 of the **ACTIVITY MANUAL** to allow students to assess how their first impressions may be impacted.

5.   Help students identify some of their own implicit theories:
   a.   Ask students to list as many "rules" or "should" statements about getting along with people as they can remember from their childhood. Some examples might be:

      Never give up.
      You can catch more flies with honey than with vinegar.
      Keep your nose to the grindstone.
      It is our duty to be cheerful.
      Share and share alike.
      The early bird catches the worm.
      Nice guys finish last.

   b.   Each student should then choose two or three of the statements and describe a situation in which that implicit theory influenced them either for good or bad.
   c.   Use **Transparency Master 3-6**. Ask students to give examples illustrating this quotation.

"Perception is not logic; it is experience."

6.   Examine self-fulfilling prophecies:

---

a. Divide students into small groups of 3-4. Ask them to share either their own or another's personal experience with self-fulfilling prophecies. In each instance, the group should identify:

> the prediction;
> the action which assumed that the prediction was true;
> the ways in which the prediction became true;
> and how the original belief was strengthened.

Each group might then share one of their examples with the rest of the class.

b. The *Skill-Building Exercise, 3.2: Perspective Taking* in **MESSAGES**, p. 67, will help students practice seeing the world through another person's perspective. Discuss possible reactions in each situation which would function to set up self-fulfilling prophecies.

7. Identify stereotypes:

a. Use **Transparency Master 3-7** on stereotypes. Ask students to name stereotypes for each of the groups listed on the transparency. You may wish to add other groups. Lighten the discomfort by introducing this exercise as one designed to insult everyone in the class. Keep asking for any group which has not been insulted.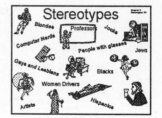

b. Assign students to interview members of various groups. They should ask:

> What is a common stereotype for your group?
> Have you felt personally stereotyped?
> How has the stereotype hurt you?
> How has it helped you?

When students bring their assignments to class, ask them to identify the groups represented in their reports. Pair students who worked with the same groups. Ask them to compare the answers they received.

c. Use *Activity 2: Disposing of Stereotypes* on p. 56 of the **ACTIVITY MANUAL** to identify professional, gender, geographical and other stereotypes.

7. Introduce attributions:

a. Invite a member of a TOUGHLOVE Parent's Support Group to speak to the class about working with children who have difficulty taking responsibility for being in control of their behavior. A counselor for adolescents could also speak to this topic.

b. Place students in groups of 3 and ask them to develop a scenario in which there are three diverse reasons to explain behavior, each one illustrating a different level of control over the situation. You may want to assign groups to work with behavior by the homeless, alcoholics, people with multiple divorces, student leaders, Greeks, and business leaders. Let the groups share their ideas with each other.

8. *Activity 1: FIPSA, Barriers to Accurate People Perception* on p. 54 of the **ACTIVITY MANUAL** will help students better understand the five processes which influence interpersonal perception.

9. Discuss the article, *What Do You Do When You Meet a Blind Person*, on pp. 69-71 of **MESSAGES**. Use the critical thinking questions at the end of the article as a guide for discussion.

10. Use the *Skill-Building Exercise 3.3: Barriers to Accurate Perception* on pp. 71-72 of **MESSAGES**.

Increasing Accuracy: Perception Checking (pp. 72-73)

Emphasis: Learning Objective 4
    Students will be able to identify the strategies for increasing accuracy in interpersonal perception.

Emphasis: Skill Objective 3
    Students will improve their abilities to use the strategies for increasing accuracy in interpersonal perception

Possible Methodologies:

1. Lecture using the information on pp. 72-73. Use **Transparency Masters 3-8** through **3-9** to visually support the material.

2. Introduce general strategies for increasing accuracy in perception. Pair all the students in the class. To the best of your ability, pair students who do not know each other. Give each pair the following assignment:
    a.   For the next three days, describe as much as you can about your partner. Keep a journal of what you observe.

---

b.   Then assign the pairs to hold a confirmation meeting. Using the guidelines on p. 72-73 of **MESSAGES**, they should both check their observations and seek to learn more about the other person.

3.   Discuss barriers to accurate people perception. Use **Transparency Master 3-9** to guide discussion.

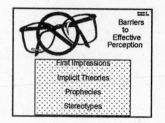

a.   Show a film such as "*Housesitter*," "*Dirty, Rotten Scoundrels*," or "*Roxanne*" with Steve Martin. In all three films there are definite misperceptions of the character Steve Martin plays.

b.   Ask students to identify specific barriers to accurate perception in the film.

4.   Assign *Activity 4: Reporter, Editor, Interviewer* on p. 60 of the **ACTIVITY MANUAL** to allow students to practice the skills of perception checking.

 Critical Thinking

Possible Methodologies:

1.   Call attention to *Critical Thinking Sidebar: Formulating Hypotheses Rather Than Conclusions* on p. 63 of **MESSAGES** by asking students to formulate three specific hypotheses related to this class or others they are in this semester. Ask them to compare their hypotheses right away with someone else in the class, and then, at the end of the class, to carefully assess whether their hypotheses were accurate.

Consider *Critical Thinking Sidebar: Look for a Variety of Cues* on p. 68 of **MESSAGES** as hypotheses are checked. What contradictory cues did the students find?

2.   Apply the skill recommendations in *Critical Thinking Sidebar: Skill Recommendations* on p. 64 of **MESSAGES** by suggesting that students find someone from a different cultural background and compare first impressions and stereotypes. What would you each need to do differently in the other culture to be interpersonally effective?

3. Discuss *Critical Thinking Sidebar: Discovery* on p. 73 of **MESSAGES**. Ask students to find someone with a very different point of view on an issue to meet with them to discuss it. What stereotypes do they find on both sides? How different are assessments of controllability related to the issue? Use **Transparency Master 3-10** to reinforce the importance of trying to understand the perspective of another person.

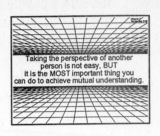

Taking the perspective of another person is not easy, BUT it is the MOST important thing you can do to achieve mutual understanding.

SKILL EVALUATION

I.   Skill Objective 1: Perceive others with the recognition that you are a major part of your own perceptions.

Use *Skill-Building Exercise 3.2: Perspective Taking*, pp. 67 of **MESSAGES**. Divide the class into five groups and assign one situation to each group. Ask the group to act out the situation to demonstrate the impact of sensing, organizing, and interpreting/evaluating.

II. Skill Objective 2: Perceive others while avoiding such common barriers as seeing what you want or expect to see, pygmalion effects, fulfilling your own predictions, seeing an individual primarily as a member of a group, mind reading, and the self-serving bias..

A.   Ask students to describe three situations demonstrating barriers to interpersonal perception. They should then analyze each for problems caused by the barrier, advantages for holding on to the barrier, and advantages for avoiding the barrier.

B.   Use *Activity 1: FIPSA, Barriers to Accurate People Perception* on p. 54 of the **ACTIVITY MANUAL** as an evaluation tool.

III. Skill Objective 3: Improve your abilities to use the strategies for increasing your accuracy in interpersonal perception.

Enlist several people to role-play characters that everyone in the class would be reasonably expected to know (the college president, yourself, television characters,

characters from a novel, etc.). The students should be given a designated period of time to observe and describe as much about the characters as possible. At the end of the designated time, provide an opportunity for students ask the characters about what they described in order to check the accuracy of their perceptions. They should then write a brief description of the character explaining how they know what they know about the person, and how they have refined their initial perceptions.

Chapter 4
LISTENING

CHAPTER OVERVIEW

We spend more time on listening than on any other communication activity, but it is not automatic or passive. It is an active process of receiving, understanding, remembering, evaluating and responding. We listen for various reasons: for enjoyment, for information, and to help. To listen effectively, we must find the balance between being participatory and passive, empathic and objective, nonjudgmental and critical, and listening on the surface or in-depth.

Active listening is a process of putting together into some meaningful whole the listener's understanding of the speaker's total message. It includes the verbal and the nonverbal, the content and the feelings. Three techniques are useful in the process of active listening: by paraphrasing the speaker's thoughts, expressing understanding of the speaker's feelings, and asking relevant questions of the speaker.

Learning Objectives

After completing this chapter, students should be able to:
1. Define *listening* and its five stages
2. Identify the five main purposes and benefits of listening
3. Identify and explain at least five obstacles to effective listening
4. Define and explain the four principles for effective listening
5. Define *active listening*, its functions, and its techniques

Skill Objectives

After completing this chapter, students should improve their abilities to:
1. Listen more effectively at each of the five stages of listening
2. Listen more effectively by avoiding the major listening barriers
3. Regulate listening on the basis of participation, empathy, judgment, and depth

4.	Respond appropriately to mixed messages
5.	Paraphrase, or put the speaker's message into their own words
6.	Listen actively and communicate this active response back

CLASSROOM APPROACHES

Introduction to Listening: (pp. 80-81)

Possible Methodologies:

1. Lecture on introductory listening information using pp. 80-81. **Transparency Master 4-1** can be used to provide an introduction.

2. Use exercise demonstrating the interpersonal impact of listening:
    a. Ask students to list the three best listeners they know. Then ask if they dislike any of the three.
    b. Ask students to list the three worst listeners they know. Ask if they like any of them.
    c. Ask students to list the characteristics of the best and worst listeners. What kind of people are they?
    d. Compare their answers with research done by Orlando Barone, Management Consultant for Sperry Univac:
        I.   Best listeners are friendly, warm, open, empathetic, honest, sincere
        ii. Worst listeners are closed, impatient, nervous, angry, unwilling to share

3. Ask students to read *Activity 5: Sound Advice for Non-Listeners* on p. 90 of the **ACTIVITY MANUAL** to reinforce information on the significance of listening.

4. Assign students to keep track of the amount of time they spend reading, speaking, writing, and listening for two days. When students bring back their statistics, put them in groups of six or seven and ask them to determine their group average for the four communication activities. Do they spend more time listening than in the other three? Were they surprised with their percentages? Compare their results with the information in Figure 4.1 on p. 81 of **MESSAGES**.

5. Use the following activity to introduce the five different purposes for listening:
   a. Divide the class into groups of five. Give each group a flipchart (or newsprint), markers and masking tape.
   b. Each group should designate a recorder.
   c. Ask each group to brainstorm as many different kinds of listening situations as they can think of. The recorder is to list all answers on the flipchart.
   d. After 3-5 minutes (or as brainstorming seems to be coming to an end), ask the groups to consider their lists and group the situations into five categories which illustrate listening for different purposes.
   e. Ask recorders for each group to post their results and report to the class on their categories.
   f. Discuss and compare the categories. Explain the five main purposes of listening on pp. 81-87. Use the class ideas to amplify the text information.

6. Use **Transparency Master 4.2** to assist in discussing *Table 4.1: The Purposes and Benefits of Effective Listening* about purposes for listening on p. 82 in **MESSAGES**. Ask students to add another example of each of the purposes for listening

7. *Activity 1: Why We Listen* on p. 81 of the **ACTIVITY MANUAL** is a good exercise to allow students to apply the information on purposes for listening to their own listening behavior.

8. Use a standardized listening test to demonstrate different purposes and types of listening. A pre-test and post-test format could also be employed to assess skill development. Possible tests include:
   a. The Brown-Carlsen Listening Comprehension Test (1955) from Harcourt, Brace & World is a standard. It measures five listening skills: immediate recall, following directions, recognizing transitions, recognizing word meanings, and lecture comprehension. It could be used to amplify the text's discussion of listening for information and to assess the student's skill levels in the areas listed.

   It can be ordered from:
   Communication Development, Inc.
   25 Robb Farm Road
   St. Paul, MN 55110
   (612) 483-3597

b. The <u>Watson-Barker Listening Test</u> was developed in 1982 and focuses on listening abilities of adults and college students. It assesses the listener's skill in evaluating message content, understanding meaning in conversations, understanding and remembering information in lectures, evaluating emotional meanings in messages, and following instructions and directions. It can be ordered from:

> Spectra Communication Associates
> P.O. Box 5031
> Contract Station 20
> New Orleans, LA 70118
> (504) 831-4440

Pfeiffer and Company has a new version (1995) of this test on video tape. It comes as **Listen Up: Skills Assessment (Form A and Form B)**, and **Listen Up: Learning Activities** with a variety of activities geared to help develop the specific listening skills assessed by the test.

The Listening Process: (pp. 81-87)

Emphasis: Learning Objectives 1 and 2
Students will be able to:
1. Define listening and its five stages.
2. Identify the five main purposes and benefits of listening.
3. Identify and explain at least five obstacles to effective listening.

Emphasis: Skill Objectives 1 and 2
Students will be able to:
1. Listen more effectively at each of the five stages of listening.
2. Listen more effectively by avoiding the major listening barriers.

Possible Methodologies:

1. Lecture on the listening processes using the information in **MESSAGES** on pp. 81-87. **Transparency Master 4-3** may be helpful to you.

2. Consider the process of receiving by demonstrating the difference between passive hearing and listening:
    a. As students come into the classroom, have a radio playing a talk show. Also be carrying on a conversation with someone.

b. To start class, turn off the radio. Ask if students heard the radio. Ask if students heard you having a conversation. Then ask them to write down what they heard on the radio and of your conversation.

c. Discuss their answers. Ask why they did not remember much of what they heard. Ask what they could have done to have received those messages more effectively.

d. Explain the difference between hearing and listening.

3. Ask students to contrast hearing and listening with an analysis of how much time they spend listening vs. hearing radio, and listening vs. hearing television.

4. Ask students to identify a major obstacle to listening which occurs during the receiving process. Which of the suggestions for making receiving more effective on pp. 82 of **MESSAGES** would be most useful in avoiding this obstacle?

5. Before the chapter is assigned for reading, present the word list on p. 85 of **MESSAGES**. Compare the class results with the results described in the text. Use **Transparency Master 4-4** for assistance.

6. Invite a memory expert to speak to the class about techniques for improving one's ability to remember.

7. Test the impact of positive vs. negative backchanneling cues by assigning half the class to give only positive cues and half the class to give only negative cues in a series of interactions they will have before the next class meeting. They are to share the responses they received at that time.

8. Assign *Skill Building Exercise 4.1: Reducing Barriers to Listening* on p. 88 of **MESSAGES.** Put students in groups of three to discuss their responses. Ask each group to share their discussion on one of the instances listed.

Effective Listening (pp. 88-96)

Emphasis: Learning Objective 4
    Students will be able to define and explain the four principles for effective listening

Emphasis: Skill Objectives 3 and 4

Students will improve their abilities to:

3.   Regulate their listening on the basis of participation, empathy, judgment, and depth
3.   Respond appropriately to mixed messages

Possible Methodologies:

1.   Lecture using information on pp. 88-96. **Transparency Masters 4-5** through **4-8** may be used to visually support the information.

2.   Introduce tips for effective listening by asking students to take the *Self-Test: "How Good a Listener Are You?"* on p. 87 of **MESSAGES**. Lead a discussion of the ideas in the Critical Thinking section following the test.

3.   Post eight signs around the room. They should read: Participatory, Passive, Empathic, Objective, Nonjudgmental, Critical, Surface and Depth. Under each sign write the question: "What does this have to do with listening?"

   As students enter class, ask them to go to each sign and write an answer to the question on it.

   When students have finished, read some of the answers to the class.   Use that information to introduce the dimensions of listening: Participation and Passive, Empathic and Objective, Nonjudgmental and Critical, Surface and Depth. Use **Transparency Master 4-5** to highlight each of the dimensions.

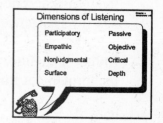

4.   Introduce the dimension of listening by asking students to list what they do when they are doing their best listening. Write their answers on a flipchart in columns corresponding to the eight listening modes..

   As you explain each of the modes, use the students' answers and add to them any techniques they have not mentioned.

5.   Participatory and Passive Listening (pp. 91-92)
   Illustrate these modes of listening by having the class do improvisations. Develop a series of stimulus situations, place students in groups of three, and, one group at a time, have one student begin making up a story from the stimulus. At a given point, call time and the second student must immediately pick up the story and continue it. Continue until all students have had several opportunities to tell parts of the story.

   Ask students to discuss participation vs. passive listening based on this experience.

Be sure students include the experience of being the audience.

6. Empathic and Objective Listening (pp. 92-94)
   a. Use *Activity 6: Creative Listening* on p. 93 of the **ACTIVITY MANUAL** to explore empathic listening skills.

   b. Ask students to watch television to find specific examples of empathic listening: listening from the speaker's point of view rather than from your own, and responding to the speaker's needs rather than your own. Discuss the examples they find in class. Use **Transparency Master 4-6** as a visual aid as you describe the concept of empathy.

Listening from the point of view of the speaker – not your own

Responding to the speaker's needs -- no your own

   c. Invite a counselor to come to speak to the class about empathic listening. What specific techniques are counselors taught to use? What is particularly useful when listening to messages which are difficult or cause strong emotional reactions? Perhaps the counselor would be willing to demonstrate empathic listening techniques.

7. Nonjudgmental and Critical Listening (p. 94)
   Illustrate leveling, sharpening and assimilation with the following exercise (similar to the old game of Gossip):
   a. Ask for 5 volunteers, four of whom leave the room. The volunteer who is still in the room is read a verbal message and instructed to repeat the message -- as accurately and as completely as possible -- to the second person. (You may wish to give a copy of the message to the rest of the class so they can identify any changes in the message.) The second person repeats the message to the third person, and so on until the fifth person repeats the message to the class.
   b. The following verbal message may be used:
   Accident Report: "I cannot wait to report this accident to the police. I must get to the hospital as soon as possible. The delivery truck, heading south, was turning right at the intersection when the sports car, heading north, attempted to turn left. When they saw that they were turning into the same lane, they both honked their horns but continued to turn without slowing down. In fact, the sports car seemed to be accelerating just before the crash."
   (from <u>Structured Experience Kit</u>, University Associates, Inc., 1980)

c. To help the class keep track of instances of leveling, sharpening and assimilation, use **Transparency Master 4-7**, "Listening for Message Distortions," as a handout or overhead transparency.

d. Discuss with the class examples of distortions. What kinds of information are distorted? Is there any sort of pattern? Does the information get more simple or more complex?

8. Surface and Depth Listening (p. 95)

a. Introduce consistency and inconsistency between verbal and non-verbal messages with the following approach. Cut a number of photographs out of magazines and/or newspapers. Distribute them to students in groups of three. Ask them to write two captions: one should capture the essence of what the people in the picture are doing; the other caption should be a contradiction to what the people in the photograph are doing. Ask groups to post their pictures and captions on the wall so that all the class can circulate around the room to see them.

b. Prepare slips of paper with the following sentences on them:
  I'm so tired I could just collapse.
  You just scared the wits out of me!
  Let me at him: I want to beat him up.
  I'm afraid I am going to fail.
  I've never tried that before.
  That is the most disgusting mess I've ever seen.
  She is the loveliest creature on earth.
  What a hunk!
  Please, please help me.
  I am thrilled to death at that news!

  I. Have students come to the front of the room, draw a slip of paper and non-verbally act out the emotion the sentence represents. The rest of the class is to guess what the emotion is. Discuss the impact of consistent messages.

  ii. Next have students draw a slip (the same sentences can be used again), and try saying the sentence while using inconsistent non-verbal behavior. Discuss the impact of the mixed messages, and the strength of the nonverbal component of the message. Use **Transparency Master 4-8** to illustrate the strength of a nonverbal message.

"Actions speak louder than words."

c. Videotape a segment from a soap opera. Play it for the class and ask them to identify content messages and relationship messages. What are some of the clues as to the relationship messages?

d. Utilize the *Skill-Building Exercise 4.2*: *Responding to Mixed Messages* on p. 96 of **MESSAGES**. Ask students to work in groups of three to identify a) the content aspect of the mixed message, b) the contradiction in the message, and c) an appropriate response to the mixed message. Ask groups to share their results.

e. Work with a small group of students to write and act out on videotape a series of mixed messages. Play the tape for the class. At the end of each example, ask the class to suggest a way to confront the mixed message.

9. A useful video for developing more effective listening skills is **How to Listen Powerfully** by CareerTrack (1-800-443-6780).

10. *Activity 7: The Power of Listening* on p. 94 of the **ACTIVITY MANUAL** guides students to think about how to listen to the whole message.

Active Listening (pp. 96-102)

Emphasis: Learning Objective 5
Students will be able to define *active listening*, its functions, and its techniques

Emphasis: Skill Objectives 5 and 6
Students will be able to:
5. Paraphrase, or put the speaker's message into their own words
6. Listen actively and communicate this active response back

Possible Methodologies:

1. Lecture using information on pp. 96-102. Use **Transparency Master 4-9** to support the information.

2. Use excerpts from the book, **How to Talk So Kids Will Listen and How to Listen So Kids Will Talk** by Adele Faber and Elaine Mazlish (Avon Books, 1980) as a stimulus to discussion. Ask the class for examples from their own experience of times when they did or did not feel listened to.

3. Use **Transparency Master 4-10** to introduce the three techniques of active listening.

4. Practice paraphrasing by bringing an assortment of Ann Landers columns and Miss Manners columns to class. Ask students to choose several items to paraphrase. After they have finished, let several students read their paraphrases to the rest of the class. The class should then give the student feedback on whether the paraphrase sounded tentative, interested, and objective.

5. Use *Skill-Building Exercise 4.3: Increasing Understanding Through Paraphrase* on p. 99 of **MESSAGES** to practice objective, accurate paraphrasing.

6. Practice expressing understanding of the speaker's feelings by using this adaptation of the standard Carl Rogers exercise:
   a. Group students by threes. Ask each group to designate a speaker, a receiver, and an observer. The speaker is to tell about a book, a movie, an experience, etc. which caused an emotional reaction. The receiver is to then reflect their understanding of the speaker's feelings as explained on pp. 100 of **MESSAGES**, and do so to the satisfaction of the speaker. The observer is to moderate, make suggestions, and keep the exercise moving.
   b. After the exercise is complete, the individuals in the group should change roles and do the exercise again until all three have played all three roles.

7. Practice asking relevant questions by playing "Press Conference." Designate a student to play the part of someone currently in the news; give the student several news clippings of a story which can be told to the rest of the class, the "reporters." The "reporters" are then to ask questions about the story (to which the student can make up answers). The first question must ask about the speaker's thoughts during

the event; the next question must deal with the speaker's emotions, and the third must ask for additional information. The "reporters" are to continue asking alternating questions until everyone has asked at least one.

8. Practice Active Listening skills by using *Activity 4: Active Listening Responses* on p. 87 of the **ACTIVITY MANUAL**. Contrast active listening skills with those of advising, evaluating and analyzing.

9. Apply active listening techniques by using *Activity 3: Active Listening: The Skill* on p. 84 of the **ACTIVITY MANUAL**.

Critical Thinking

Possible Methodologies:

1. Use *Critical Thinking Sidebar 4.1: Men and Women as Listeners* on p. 88 of **MESSAGES** for discussion. Ask students what their experience is regarding men and women in conversation. Assign them to observe several conversations to see whether they confirm or deny Deborah Tannen's conclusions. They should include the information in *Critical Thinking Sidebar 4.3: Women and Men as Active Listeners* on p. 98 of **MESSAGES** as well.

2. After reading the article, *Want To Do Better On The Job? Listen Up!*, on p. 89 of **MESSAGES**, ask students to discuss their own experiences in jobs. Ask them to consciously practice the suggestions for effective listening and assess their impact at work.

3. Apply the ideas from *Critical Thinking Sidebar 4.2: Listening for Truth and Accuracy* on p. 93 of **MESSAGES** by asking students to attend a meeting of the Student Senate, the Faculty Senate, the City Council, County Court, or a political rally. They should practice listening critically and share their observations at the next class meeting.

4. Use the questions in *Critical Thinking Sidebar 4.4: Discovery* on p. 101 of **MESSAGES** as a survey. Ask students to each ask ten people to respond to the questions. At the next class meeting, have them compare notes to see whether they are finding any kind of consensus among the responses.

5. Encourage students to continue journaling their experiences. Guidance for a focus on listening can be found in *Activity 8: Messages and Me* on p. 98 of the **ACTIVITY MANUAL** .

SKILL EVALUATION

I. Skill Objective 1: Listen more effectively at each of the five stages of listening

    A. Place students in pairs. Give them a topic of conversation. As they discuss, ask them to identify what they are doing to listen more effectively at each stage of the listening process.

    B. Ask each student to observe two other students in conversation and coach them through the five stages of listening.

II. Skill Objective 2: Listen more effectively by avoiding the major listening barriers

    A. Video or audio-tape a group playing the "gossip" game described above under "Nonjudgmental and Critical Listening." Use a story not used in class.

    Play the tape for the class. Ask: List all instances of leveling, sharpening, assimilation and other listening barriers.

    B. Ask students to read *Activity 6: Creative Listening* on p. 93 of the **ACTIVITY MANUAL** and then describe the characteristics of a creative listener they know.

    C. Use *Activity 2: Effective Listening Prescription* on p. 83 of the **ACTIVITY MANUAL** as an evaluation tool.

III. Skill Objective 3: Regulate listening on the basis of participation, empathy, judgment, and depth

    A. Schedule students in pairs. Their assignment for the skill evaluation is to plan and present a conversation within which they will demonstrate listening with participation, empathy, judgment, and depth.

They should hand in a written script identifying all the skills listed.

B. Choose topics about which students would be likely to have strong feelings. Pair students with opposing views, or ask them to role-play opposing views. Each individual in the pair will be asked to present his/her position while the other individual demonstrates at least three empathic listening techniques.

IV. Skill Objective 4: Respond appropriately to mixed messages

Play a videotaped segment illustrating mixed messages. Ask the students to identify non-verbal inconsistencies, and content and relationship issues. Then ask them what they would say to confront the mixed message in a non-threatening way.

V. Skill Objective 5: Paraphrase, or put the speaker's message into your own words

Play an audio tape of a short speech. Ask students to paraphrase three main ideas in the speech. This evaluation may be done either orally or in writing.

VI. Skill Objective 6: Listen actively and communicate this active response back

A. Express understanding of the speaker's feelings: Read the following comments and at the conclusion of each, have the students write the way they would express understanding of the speaker's feelings.

"I just found out that I didn't get the job that I applied for. I can't believe it; she as much as promised that I would get it."

"Without that job, I might as well quit school. There is no way I can pay all my bills."

"I dread having to tell my parents. I know they will offer to help, but I don't want them to. I said I was going to support myself, and I intend to do it."

B. Divide the class into groups of six or seven. Ask them to write a short funny skit based on some current event in the vicinity. Require that the skit be a parody including some emotional statements and some mixed messages. The students should give an exaggerated demonstration of paraphrasing, expressing understanding of the speaker's feelings, and asking questions.

Each time that the "actors" demonstrate one of the techniques for active listening, the students in the audience should respond: call out the technique, throw popcorn, boo/hiss, cheer, etc.

C. Use *Skill-Building Exercise 4.4: Using Active Listening* on pp. 101-102 of **MESSAGES** as a evaluation tool for active listening skills.

Chapter 5
COMMUNICATING VERBALLY

CHAPTER OVERVIEW

It is through language that we communicate meanings, the most significant function of communication. Some important principles of meaning include:

Meanings are denotative and connotative.
Meanings are in people.
Meanings depend on context.
Meanings are packaged.

Barriers to effective thinking and verbal communication include polarization, intensional orientation, fact-inference confusion, allness, static evaluation, and indiscrimination.

Linguistic racism, sexism, and heterosexism are all forms of disconfirming communication. Confirming communication accepts, supports, and acknowledges the importance of the other person.

Learning Objectives

After completing this chapter, students should be able to:
1. Identify the characteristics of meaning and their implications for human communication
2. Define and provide examples of the barriers to thinking and communicating
3. Explain disconfirmation and distinguish it from confirmation and rejection
4. Explain the nature of racism, sexism, and heterosexism

Skill Objectives

After completing this chapter, students should improve their abilities to:
1. Construct and respond to messages as both connotative and denotative, as in people rather than only in words, as dependent on context, as packaged, and as rule-governed
2. Avoid the common misevaluations in thinking and in communicating
3. Use confirming responses as appropriate while avoiding racist, sexist, and heterosexist language

CLASSROOM APPROACHES

Meaning in Interpersonal Communication (pp. 110-118)

Emphasis: Learning Objective 1
Students will be able to identify the characteristics of meaning and their implications for human communication.

Emphasis: Skill Objective 1
Students will be able to construct and respond to messages as both connotative and denotative, as in people rather than only in words, as dependent on context, as packaged, and as rule-governed.

Possible Methodologies:
1. Lecture using the information on pp. 110 - 118. Use **Transparency Masters 5-1** and **5-2** to visually support your information.

2. Divide students into groups of six or seven. Ask each group to write a dialogue based on a situation such as the introductory one found on p. 110 in **MESSAGES**. For each comment made in the dialogue, there should be a parenthetical explanation of the meaning intended in order to illustrate the principle that meanings are both denotative and connotative. It might be fun to have the groups act out their

dialogues.

3.   Introduce the principle of looking for meanings in people and not in words with a brief "test." Ask students to write the first meaning that comes to mind for each of the following words:

        a. son
        b. bear
        c. abortion
        d. Democrat
        e. Gore
        f. pica
        g. aglet

Word by word, ask for examples for the meanings people assigned to words. Comment on the variety. Some of the reasons for the differences relate to the following concepts:

Homonyms: Words a and b are examples of words which sound alike but have different meanings. While these may cause some difficulty in communication, context usually solves the problems.

Connotations: Words c and d are examples of words for which there are strong emotional reactions. Discuss the emotions implied by the various meanings assigned by the class.

Context: Word e is another homonym (Al Gore or gore). The meaning assigned was probably strongly influenced by the context set by the preceding word.

Substitution: The word "pica" refers to a strange craving for unusual things to eat such as chalk or ash. Students are likely to assume that they have heard the words "pick up" or "pick a" or "pica" (a typeface). Discuss the difficulties which arise when two people mistakenly think they share a meaning.

Semantic Blanks: The word "aglet" refers to the hard end of a shoelace. Only the rare student will know what it is. There may be some humorous substitutions, but almost uniformly students will know that they do not know the real meaning. Discuss how knowing that you do not know can lead to meaningful interactions.

4.   Ask students to fill out the chart on p. 112 of **MESSAGES**. Place students in groups to compare responses and illustrate the different meanings in people and the impact of connotations.

5.   *Activity 1: Descending the Abstraction Ladder* on p. 106 of the **ACTIVITY MANUAL** provides additional practice on dealing with abstract and concrete language as does *Skill-Building Exercise 5.1: Climbing the Abstraction Ladder* on pp. 113-114 of **MESSAGES**.

6.   Use **Transparency Master 5-2** for examples of abstractions and specificity.

8.   Ask students to write five different examples of the same words being used in two different contexts and their meanings being influenced by those contexts. An example you might provide is: "We have a great problem with nurses and aides." The two contexts are a hospital administrative meeting and a discussion at the local AIDS Outreach Center. How will "aides" be interpreted in each?

9.   Assign the same exercise as that above, only this time ask that the contexts be culturally different.

10.   Ask that students "collect" three examples of actual instances in which the verbal and nonverbal messages contradict each other. Describe the ways in which the messages conflict. In addition, students should collect three examples of messages which function together. In each case, they should identify, according to Knapp and Hall (p. 115 of **MESSAGES**) exactly how the messages are packaged.

11.   Ask student to choose one of the two articles, *Interpersonal Messages in the Organization* on pp. 116-117, or *How to Talk to the Opposite Sex* on p. 117-118 of **MESSAGES** and apply it to their own experiences. What specific examples can they share to illustrate the principles in the article?

Barriers in Thinking and Communicating (pp. 118-127)

Emphasis: Learning Objective 2
        Students will be able to define and provide examples of the barriers to thinking

and communicating

Emphasis: Skill Objective 2
Students will improve their abilities to avoid the common misevaluations in thinking and in communicating

Possible Methodologies:

1.   Lecture using the information on pp. 118 - 127. Use **Transparency Masters 5-3** through **5-8** to visually support the information.

Each of the Transparency Masters for this section include both a definition/example of a barrier to clear language, and a suggestion/example for avoiding the barrier. You may wish to cover the bottom half of the transparency while you discuss the barrier. Ask for suggestions for avoiding the barrier before revealing the bottom half of the transparency.

2.   Use *Skill-Building Exercise 5.2: Polarizing Language* on p. 120 of **MESSAGES** to illustrate the difficulty of avoiding polarization.

3.   Assign students to listen for and record twelve example of polarizing language in everyday conversation. Report on these in class and discuss the impact of the language on the interactions observed. Use **Transparency Master 5-3.**

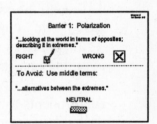

4.   In an effort to help students avoid polarizing, assign *Activity 3: Triangles with Meaning* on p. 110 of the **ACTIVITY MANUAL.**

5.   To demonstrate an intensional orientation, set up a table of refreshments for the class. Include some of the following food and labels:

two plates of hamburger patties with one labeled "hamburger" and the other "ground-up dead cow"

two plates of frankfurters with one labeled "hot dogs" and the other labeled with the list of ingredients from the package

two containers of yogurt with one labeled "yogurt" and the other labeled "a jellylike substance fermented by bacterial action" two containers of caviar with one labeled "caviar" and the other labeled "fish eggs"

Other possibilities could include headcheese, sweetmeats, fake chocolate, an alcoholic beverage, radishes, turnip greens, etc.

Ask students to pick what they would like to eat. Compare choices and reactions. Discuss the impact of labels. Use **Transparency Master 5-4**.

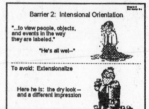

6. Divide the class into four groups. Set up a contest among the groups over which one can name the most destructive labels used in everyday conversation in five minutes. Then give five minutes for the most positive labels they can name.

7. Before discussing fact-inference confusion, use the *Self Test: Can you Distinguish Facts from Inferences?* on p. 121 of **MESSAGES**. Grade the test to demonstrate how easily we confuse facts and inferences. Use **Transparency Master 5-5** as you discuss ways of avoiding fact-inference confusion.

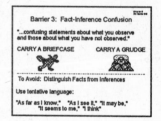

8. Ask students to name several people they knew in grade school and with whom they still have contact. What evaluations did they make of those friends back in school? Is there a tendency to hang on to those evaluations? How hard is it to remember that people grow up and change? Ask students to make two statements about each of the friends listed. Date the statements for grade school days and for now. Use **Transparency Master 5-6** as you discuss static evaluation.

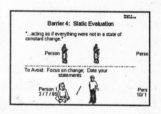

9. *Activity 2: Old Words, New Words* on p. 109 of the **ACTIVITY MANUAL** will help students consider how words as well as meanings and referents change over time.

10. Assign students to spend one whole day working on correcting allness. They should end every declarative statement with the word "etcetera," and follow that

up by attempting to add what that "etcetera" might be. Report at the next class meeting on how that felt and any new insights it gave. Use **Transparency Master 5-7** for support.

11. Inform students about **ETC: A Review of General Semantics**, and how its name illustrates the effort to avoid allness.

12. Use **Transparency Master 5-8** for an example of indiscrimination and of indexing.

13. *Activity 4: Wording* on p. 112 of the **ACTIVITY MANUAL** provides an opportunity for a good review of this section and for practice of correcting barriers in thinking and communicating.

14. Practice identifying the barriers to clear thinking and clear language by using *Skill-Building Exercise 5.2: Combating Barriers to Clear Thinking and Clear Language* on pp. 124-125 in **MESSAGES**. After students have completed the exercise, group them and ask the groups to discuss their analysis of the barriers. In a large group discussion, ask the groups to share some of their ideas.

15. After students read the article, *"10 Things You Should Never Say to Anyone,"* on pp. 125-127 of **MESSAGES**, ask them to spend a week listening for examples of those very statements. Can they think of ways to respond to those statements to reduce the negative impact they have? *Activity 5: Paying Attention to Words* on p. 117 of the **ACTIVITY MANUAL** also helps students make wise word choices.

Disconfirmation (pp. 127 - 135)

Emphasis: Learning Objectives 3 and 4
   Students will be able to:
   3.   Explain disconfirmation and distinguish it from confirmation and rejection
   4.   Explain the nature of language racism, sexism, and heterosexism.

Emphasis: Skill Objective 3
   Students will improve their abilities to use confirming responses as appropriate

while avoiding racist, sexist, and heterosexist language

Possible Methodologies:

1. Lecture using information on pp. 127-135. Use **Transparency Master 5-9**.

Disconfirmation

Language Racism - used by members of one culture to disparage members of other cultures

Language Sexism - Generic "man" Generic "he" and "his" Sex role stereotyping

Language Heterosexism - used to disparage gay men and lesbians

2. In addition to having students take the *Self-Test: How Confirming Are You?* On pp. 127-128 of **MESSAGES**, assign them to ask three to five friends and family members to answer the questions about them. Are their responses consistent with the student's self assessment? If not, why might this be? If so, why? What information or conclusions do the students gain from this exercise?

3. Use *Table 5.1: Confirmation Versus Disconfirmation* on p. 129 of **MESSAGES** to ask students to find examples of as many of the ways to confirm and to disconfirm as they can.

4. *Training Magazine*, Vol. 13, No. 4, has an excellent article, "Toward More Authentic Interpersonal Relations Between Blacks and Whites," by Bertram Lee and Warren Schmidt. It lists assumptions and behaviors by whites which block authentic relations with blacks; it lists assumptions and behaviors by blacks which block authentic relations with whites. It also lists assumptions and behaviors which facilitate authentic relations.

5. There is a wonderful "test" to measure your sexism quotient in the May/June 1980 issue of *The Columbia Journalism Review*. It demonstrates how even professional communicators get caught with sexist presumptions. Students will find that some of the items on the test are difficult for them because of their own sexist presumptions. It makes a good introduction to a discussion of linguistic sexism.

6. An excellent resource is the booklet, ***On Equal Terms: How to Eliminate Sexism in Communications*** published by the Communications Branch of the Correctional Service of Canada (340 Laurier Avenue West, Ottawa Ontario K1A OP9).

    An additional helpful resource is "Removing Bias: Guidelines for Student-Faculty Communication" by Mercilee M. Jenkins, major contributing author, in *Sex and*

Gender in the Social Sciences by Judith M. Gappa and Janice Pearce (Annandale, Virginia: Speech Communication Association, 1983).

7.   Assign the following experiment: Ask students to write a series of five descriptive statements using one of the following sets of instructions:
   a)   Use all masculine generic pronouns, and then re-write each sentence using inclusive language. They are then to read the sentences to ten children, separately, under the age of seven and ask each child to tell a little about the person or event being described. Record how many times the masculine generic sentences elicit descriptions with males in them as opposed to the inclusive sentences.
   b)   Use language which is all related to whites, and then re-write using language related to blacks. Read the statements to 10 different people and ask them to describe the people in your statements. Make note of what race the people are assumed to be in each set of statements.
   c)   Use language presupposing heterosexist attitudes. Read the statements to 10 people and ask them to describe the people in your statements. Is a sexual orientation mentioned? If not, ask what sexual orientation is assumed. How often is a gay orientation assumed?

8.   Suggest students read the book, **Stranger at the Gate: To Be Gay and Christian in America**, by Mel White (Simon & Schuster, 1994) to explore the impact of instances of heterosexist language and behavior.

9.   Other possible books for discussion are **Gayspeak** edited by James Chesebro (Pilgrim Press, 1981), and **Heterosexism: An Ethical Challenge** by Patricia Beattie Jung and Ralph F. Smith (SUNY Press, 1993).

10.   Use *Activity 6: Languages from Venus and Mars* on p. 123 of the **ACTIVITY MANUAL** to explore the gender gap in communication.

Critical Thinking

Possible Methodologies:
1.   Use the dialogue on pp. 118-119 of **MESSAGES** as a stimulus to a critical thinking activity. Ask students to explore the concept that distortions in thought lead to distortions in language, and distortions in language (because we think in and with our language) further distort our thinking. Can they find examples of

either of those distortions? Is it even possible to examine the relationship between thinking and language thoroughly since our thinking is so bound by language?

2. Related to *Skill-Building Exercise 5.3: Combating Barriers to Clear Thinking and Clear Language,* ask students to spend some time identifying five ideas which they absolutely believe. Can they assure themselves that they have not inadvertently been influenced by one of the barriers to clear thinking?

3. Use the questions in the critical thinking box on *Discovery* on p. 135 of **MESSAGES**. Ask students to write responses to each question and then discuss them in class.

4. Working with words in the process of journaling will be a helpful way to apply ideas from this chapter. Use *Activity 7: Messages and Me* on p. 128 of the **ACTIVITY MANUAL**.

SKILL EVALUATION

I. Skill Objective 1: Construct and respond to messages as both connotative and denotative, as in people rather than only in words, as dependent on context, as packaged, and as rule-governed

Collect a variety of newspaper headlines. Ask students to provide at least two different meanings for each. What are the denotations and connotations of specific words in the headlines which lead to the different meanings? How do context and packaging influence meanings? (An enjoyable way to do this evaluation would be to use examples of headlines from the "The Lower Case" in each issue of *The Columbia Journalism Review*. These are always funny instances of ambiguity and multiple meanings. Several have been reproduced for you on **Transparency Master 5-10**. Use a reveal technique as you show them to the class.)

II. Skill Objective 2: Avoid the common misevaluations in thinking and in communicating

Use *Activity 4: Wording* on p. 112 of the **ACTIVITY MANUAL** as an evaluation tool covering all of the barriers to effective communication.

III. Skill Objective 3:   Use confirming responses as appropriate while avoiding racist, sexist, and heterosexist language

    A.   Provide examples of writing with racist, sexist, and/or heterosexist language and ask students to re-write them inclusively. Some sources to look for examples include hymns, political speeches from the past, legal language, old newspaper articles, etc.

    B.   Use *Skill-Building Exercise 5.4: Expressing Confirmation, Rejection, and Disconfirmation* of **MESSAGES** as an evaluation tool. In addition to following the instructions as written, also ask students to provide confirming, rejecting and disconfirming responses to the examples under the "Thinking Critically" section of the exercise on p. 131.

Chapter 6
COMMUNICATING NONVERBALLY

CHAPTER OVERVIEW

Nonverbal communication, communication without words, occurs in the following forms:
> body language (emblems, illustrators, affect displays, regulators, and adaptors),
> facial and eye communication
> spatial and territorial communication
> artifactual communication
> touch communication
> paralanguage or the sound of our voices
> silence, and
> time communication.

Learning Objectives

After completing this chapter, students should be able to:
1. Define and provide examples of five kinds of body movements
2. Describe the types of information communicated by the face and eyes
3. Explain the four distances
4. Define territoriality and marker
5. Explain artifactual communication and how color, clothing, and space decoration communicate messages
6. Explain the major meanings communicated by touch
7. Define paralanguage and its role in making judgments about people and effectiveness
8. Explain the major functions of silence
9. Explain how time communicates and the concepts of cultural and psychological time
10. Explain why the interpretations of nonverbal messages are influenced by culture

---

CLASSROOM APPROACHES

Introduction to Nonverbal Communication (p. 141-142)

Possible Methodologies:
1.   Introduce the chapter by conducting an entire class nonverbally. (Or maybe a portion of the class!) Use **Transparency Master 6-1** to alert the class to what is happening.

There are several ways you might conduct the class:

a.   One suggestion would be to set up learning centers around the room. The different areas could have such emphases as posters showing various forms of nonverbal communication, a slide show with music, an assortment of costumes and uniforms, a variety of unusual things to feel, a silent movie, someone signing for the deaf, a mime, etc. After students have had a chance to experience all of the centers, discuss their conclusions about nonverbal communication. Use

---

Transparency Master 6-2 to illustrate various kinds of nonverbal communication.

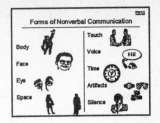

b.   A second approach might be to present a series of nonverbal messages to the class as a whole. Some of the same suggestions for the centers could be used in such a way as to present a logical, sequential message about nonverbal communication.   At the conclusion of the presentation, ask students for their interpretations of the message. Discuss similarities and differences in interpretation and why these might have occurred.

2.   *Activity 4: Body Signals from Live for Success* on p. 155 of the **ACTIVITY MANUAL** provides an overview of the significance of nonverbal communication.

3.   Assign students to spend a set period of time without using any verbal communication. They should rely on nonverbal communication and record their feelings about it as well as the reactions they receive.

4.   To illustrate that nonverbal behaviors communicate, show a silent movie and ask the class what the story is. Or show a sequence of pictures. **Life Magazine** has wonderful pictorial essays you could show. Discuss with the class the clarity of the story as it is shown nonverbally.

5.   Review the suggestions for studying nonverbal communication on p. 142 of **MESSAGES**. Develop a self assessment format for students to use: list each of the forms of nonverbal communication and provide space for comments. Give each student three copies of the sheet and ask them to ask three good friends to make comments about their use of each of the nonverbal forms. You might have the students share responses in class. Ask students to set some specific goals to work on related to the feedback they receive.

Body Movements (pp. 142-143)

Emphasis: Learning Objective 1
Students will be able to define and provide examples of five kinds of body movements

Emphasis: Skill Objective 1
> Students will be able to use a wide variety of nonverbal communication forms to encode and decode meanings.

Possible Methodologies:

1. Lecture using the information on pp. 142-143 of **MESSAGES**. Use **Transparency Master 6-3** for support.

2. To begin discussing body language, make slides from pictures found in magazines, newspapers, etc., which show examples of emblems, illustrators, affect displays, regulators, and adaptors. Use these as you discuss each of the categories. Use **Transparency Master 6-3** for support.

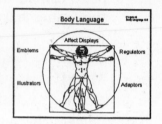

3. Divide the class into five groups and assign one of the types of body language to each group. Ask them to act out for the class three instances of their assigned category.

4. Assign students to collect instances of each of the categories over the following 48 hours. Which category is the most frequent?

5. Illustrate emblems by inviting a person who signs for the deaf to speak to the class about signing and to demonstrate it. While signing is not vocal, it is related to verbal communication; discuss the connection.

6. If you have any scuba divers or radio/TV majors in your class, ask them to share the emblems they use in their particular contexts.

7. Assign a designated period of time during which students may not use any illustrators. Discuss the difficulty of verbal communication without nonverbal support.

8. Assign students to experiment with using positive and negative regulators. What impact do they have on the speaker?

9. Put students in pairs and assign them to assess each other's adaptors. After they

collect information and instances for several days, they should meet with each other and discuss their observations. It may be appropriate for them to discuss which adaptors send negative information about the sender.

Facial and Eye Movements (pp. 143-148)

Emphasis: Learning Objective 2
Students will be able to describe the types of information communicated by the face and the eyes.

Emphasis: Skill Objective 2
Students will improve their abilities to use facial and eye cues to receive and send information.

Possible Methodologies:

1.   Lecture using information from pp. 143-148. Use **Transparency Masters 6-4 and 6-5** for support.

2.   Research information from the old schools of oratory when facial expressions were meticulously defined and learned. Share this information with the class.

3.   The schools of oratory taught that there are 27 different eyebrow positions. Find an assortment of pictures with various eyebrow positions. You may want to make them into slides. Discuss how we use eyebrows to signal meaning.

4.   Show a series of pictures or slides of various facial expressions, or use **Transparency Master 6-4**. Discuss what emotion is demonstrated. Check to see what kind of consistency the class has as they assign emotional meaning. Discuss how similarly we interpret nonverbal signals.

5.   Use *Table 6.1: Facial Management Techniques* on p. 145 of **MESSAGES** to discuss how we learn to send specific facial messages.

6.   Divide students into groups each of which is assigned one of the major functions of eye communication. Each group should develop a brief skit demonstrating its assigned function. Use **Transparency Master 6-5**.

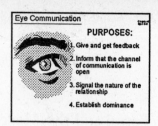

7.   Ask students to find references to eye communication in literature. Share them with the class. Categorize each instance according to the four functions.

8.   Use item 5 in the *Critical Thinking* section on p. 151 of **MESSAGES** to examine differences in eye communication between American blacks and American whites. Discuss the conclusions students draw from their experiences.

Spatial and Territorial Communication (pp. 148-152)

Emphasis: Learning Objectives 3 and 4
        Students will be able to:
        3.   Explain the four distances
        4.   Define territoriality and marker

Emphasis: Skill Objective 3
        Student will improve their abilities to use spatial distance and markers to communicate their intended meanings

Possible Methodologies:

1.   Lecture using information on pp. 148-152. Use **Transparency Master 6-6** for support.

2.   To begin a discussion of space communication, rearrange the classroom so that no one can sit in an accustomed place. Discuss the impact of the changed space.

3.   If you spend several class meetings on space communication, change the room for each meeting. Vary from a very formal arrangement to one with no chairs at all to one with scattered seating. Discuss how the arrangements influence class interactions.

4. Use *Skill-Building Exercise 6.2: Interacting in Space* on p. 151 of **MESSAGES** as a demonstration of the use of space. Ask students to observe actual interactions in a public area and assess the relationships demonstrated by them.

5. Find pictures of people in each of the four distances. Use **Transparency Master 6-6**. Show them to the class and ask what sort of relationship each implies for the people involved.

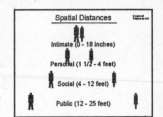

6. Use the following little poem by W. H. Auden to introduce the idea of personal space:

> Some thirty inches from my nose,
> The frontier of my person goes.
> And all the untilled air between
> Is private pagus or demesne.
> Stranger, unless with bedroom eyes
> I beckon you to fraternize,
> Beware of rudely crossing it.
> I have no gun but I can spit!

7. Assign students to record instances they encounter of each of the four distances. In what circumstances do they occur? How does the distance influence the interactions?

8. To illustrate territoriality, assign students to choose a class or a church group and map where individuals in those groups sit at each meeting of the group. To what extent do people begin to "own" their space? Interview a minister concerning the seating patterns of the congregation. What happens when someone violates the traditional seating patterns?

9. Research (or assign students to do so) information in education literature concerning the impact of location in the classroom with success in the class. Ask students to apply it to their own experiences.

10. Assign students to collect instances of markers to share with the class.

11. Ask students how they mark their own territory. What is "staked out" in their

homes: a bedroom, a chair, the kitchen?

Artifactual Communication (pp. 153-156)

Emphasis: Learning Objective 5
Students will be able to explain artifactual communication and how color, clothing, and space decoration communicate messages.

Emphasis: Skill Objective 4
Students will improve their abilities to decode the possible meanings of artifacts and use artifacts to communicate their own meanings.

Possible Methodologies:

1. Lecture using the information on pp. 153-156. Use **Transparency Master 6-7** for support.

2. Begin discussing artifactual communication by asking students how they use color in their clothes and homes. Why do they like the colors they like?

3. Ask an interior decorator and/or designer to speak to the class about the impact of color in living and working spaces.

4. Assign *Skill-Building Exercise 6.3: Communicating with Colors* on pp. 153-154 of **MESSAGES**. Place students in groups of three to compare their color choices and reasoning. What commonalities do they find? Are there any consistent differences?

5. Interview a group of junior high girls about what clothes are important to wear. Interview a group of high school boys about what cars are important to drive. What do their comments say about the significance of artifactual communication?

6. Collect advertisements for perfume and cologne (or ask students to collect them). What messages are being sent by these smells?

7. Assign students to interview the sales people at a perfume counter of a department

store. How do people make their decisions about which scent to buy? How do the store's buyers make their decisions about which scents to stock?

8. Collect several "dress for success" books (John Malloy's **Dress for Success,** Warner Books, 1975; Malloy's **Woman's Dress for Success**, Warner Books, 1977; **Executive Style: Looking It, Living It** created by Mary B. Fiedorek and written by Diana Lewis Jewell, New Century Publishers, Inc., 1983**).** Display them so that students can look through them. After they have examined them, discuss: what is the basic premise on which the books are based? How significant is one's appearance to one's success? Are the guidelines in the books consistent, or are there divergent messages? Do the guidelines change over time, or are there some unchanging principles?

9. Collect pictures of several famous people (Princess Di, Einstein, Abraham Lincoln, George Washington, Willie Nelson, Hillary Clinton, Michael Jackson, etc.). Cut out their faces so that you have only their hairstyles left. Make a handout or a transparency of these hairstyles. (You can call this "Hairstyles of the Rich and Famous!") Ask students to identify the people by their hairstyles. Discuss the messages sent by these various styles.

10. Assign students to interview a set designer for a theatre. How are stage arrangements and set decorations used to convey a message?

11. Ask students to visit a large business with offices in one building. Ask them to identify the status of various positions within the company by analyzing the offices and their furnishings.

12. Use *Activity 1: Nonverbal Fieldwork* on p. 141 of the **ACTIVITY MANUAL** to assist students to notice the range of artifactual communication.

Touch Communication (pp. 156-157)

Emphasis: Learning Objective 6
Students will be able to explain the major meanings communicated by touch.

Emphasis: Skill Objectives 5 and 6
> Students will improve their abilities to:
>   5.   Use touch cues to send and receive meaning
>   6.   Respond appropriately to touch avoidance cues

Possible Methodologies:
1.   Lecture using information on pp. 156-157 of **MESSAGES**. **Transparency Master 6-8** is an appropriate visual aid.

2.   On the day you are going to discuss touch communication, greet each student at the door with a hug (or a handshake, if you are uncomfortable with a hug). Discuss how that felt.

3.   Use *Activity 2: What's Shakin'?* on p. 144 of the **ACTIVITY MANUAL** to examine handshakes as a form of touch communication.

4.   Ask students who grew up in homes where there was a lot of touching to group together. Form another group of those who grew up in homes where there was not a lot of touching. Ask each group to brainstorm about acceptable and unacceptable touching behavior. Compare lists. What kinds of touch avoidance behavior has each group encountered?

5.   Ask students to make a pledge that they will give and/or receive at least 4 hugs a day for a week. They are then to assess how they felt about it. To what extend did they encounter touch avoidance reactions? You may want to assign a research project on hugging. Students should look up information from Greg Risberg, Leo Buscaglia and Sidney Simon.

Paralanguage (pp. 157-159)

Emphasis: Learning Objective 7
> Students will be able to define paralanguage and its role in making judgments about people and effectiveness

Emphasis: Skill Objective 7
> Students will improve their abilities to use paralanguage to encode and decode intended meanings

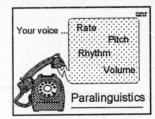

Possible Methodologies:
1. Lecture using the information on pp. 157-159 of **MESSAGES**. Use **Transparency Master 6-9** for support.

2. Use **Transparency Master 6-10** to introduce paralanguage with the following sentence:
   > "I would not say you lost the fight."

   Read it seven different times with an emphasis on a different word each time. Each time ask the students what the meaning is. Consider the change in meaning resulting from the change in paralanguage.

3. Assign students to pay particular attention to the paralanguage of their professors. Analyze its impact on the classes. Which characteristic (rate, pitch, volume, or rhythm) seems to be the most significant?

4. Try a content-free language exercise. List a number of different emotions on separate small sheets of paper. Ask students to each draw one out, and then to make sounds (NOT words) to convey their emotion. The rest of the class is to guess which emotion it is.

5. Use *Skill-Building Exercise 6.4: Praising and Criticizing* on p. 159 in **MESSAGES** to analyze the impact of paralanguage on whether a message is received positively or negatively.

Silence (pp. 160-161)

Emphasis: Learning Objective 8
> Students will be able to explain the major functions of silence.

Emphasis: Skill Objective 8
> Students will improve their abilities to use silence signals to send and receive

intended meanings.

Possible Methodologies:

1. Lecture using the information on pp. 160-161. Use **Transparency Master 6-11**.

2. Assign students to watch a movie of their choice and to analyze the uses and functions of silence in it.

3. Assign students to remain silent for a specified amount of time during their regular interactions before the next class. What are the reactions of other people?

4. During one class meeting, plan a specified period of silence. Afterwards, ask students to analyze their reaction to it. How often do they experience silence? How comfortable are they with it?

5. Ask students to assess their own experience with silence. Where do they encounter it: Religious services? Club rituals? With strangers? Library? Other?

Time Communication (pp. 161-164)

Emphasis: Learning Objective 9
Student will be able to explain how time communicates and the concepts of cultural and psychological time.

Emphasis: Skill Objectives 9 and 10
Students will improve their abilities to
9.   Clarify informal time terms
10. Interpret time cues from a cultural perspective

Possible Methodologies:

1. Lecture on the information on pp. 161-164 of **MESSAGES**. Use **Transparency Master 6-12**.

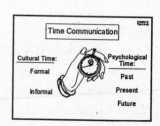

2. Give students the *Test Yourself: What Time Do You*

Have? on pp. 162-164 of **MESSAGES**. Students should assess their own scores in order to find out their orientation to each of the seven factors. Ask students to give the test to their spouse or best friend. How similar are their orientations? What kinds of problems might they anticipate?

3.   Invite someone from another culture to speak to the class about differences in time expectations. Use **Transparency Master 6-12**.

4.   Assign students to interview a dozen people about informal time. Each should be asked to estimate the length of time for each of the following:

> soon
> immediately
> as soon as possible
> in a little while
> right away
> in a minute

How varied are the responses? How might communication problems over informal time be avoided?

Culture and Nonverbal Communication (pp. 166-167)

Emphasis: Learning Objective 10
Student will be able to explain why the interpretation of nonverbal messages are influenced by culture.

Emphasis: Skill Objective 11
Students will improve their abilities to use nonverbal behaviors with an awareness of cultural differences and influences.

Possible Methodologies:
1.   Lecture over the information on pp. 166-167 of **MESSAGES**.

2.   Invite some international students to speak to the class about nonverbal behaviors they found surprising when they first came to this culture.

3.   Discuss the context of nonverbal messages by asking students who have traveled in other countries to give examples of nonverbal behaviors they found unusual.

4.   Put students in small groups and ask them to plan a short demonstration of nonverbal behavior which would vary widely in its interpretation in different contexts. They should present it to the whole class by setting the first context, doing the scene, and then setting the second context and doing the scene again. Discuss how context influences meaning.

5.   An excellent group of books on the impact of culture on nonverbal communication were written by Roger E. Axtell. They include *Gestures: the Do's and Taboos of Body Language Around the World*, *Do's and Taboos Around the World*, *Do's and Taboos of Hosting International Visitors*, and *The Do's and Taboos of International Trade*. All are published by John Wiley.

6.   John T. Molloy's book, *Live for Success*, Bantam Books, 1981, has an excellent discussion of effective and ineffective nonverbal behavior. Malloy relates effective nonverbal behavior to a set of standards practiced by people in upper socio-economic classes. Are these rules? Might they be used as rules?

7.   Ask students to assess the nonverbal rules they grew up with. What are some examples? (Stand up when an adult enters the room, don't shake hands with a lady unless she initiates it, don't speak unless spoken to, families hug and kiss on the lips--or they don't, signs of affection are appreciated--or not, etc.)

8.   Discuss *Table 6.2: A Few Nonverbals That Can Get You Into Trouble* on p. 167 of **MESSAGES**.

 Critical Thinking

Possible Methodologies:
1.   Consider sex differences in nonverbal communication. Use *Critical Thinking Sidebar: Sex Differences* on p. 142 to guide the discussion.

2.   Guide students to think about the variety of interpretations of nonverbal signals. The *Critical Thinking Sidebar: Accuracy in Reading Nonverbal Signals* on p. 152 will help focus thinking. Check out some of the popular books on nonverbal communication such as **Body Language** and look for conflicting advice.

3.   Assign student to analyze nonverbal behavior by using the *Critical Thinking Sidebar: Accuracy in Detecting Lying* on p. 164. Have them choose some other emotion or behavior other than lying and see if they can find consistent nonverbal signals related to that emotion or behavior.

4.   The article *Safety Signage* on p. 165 of **MESSAGES** looks at graphic symbols. Discuss the questions at the end of the article. What other graphic symbols do the students think of? How effective are they?

5.   Place students in five groups and assign one of the questions in the *Critical Thinking Sidebar: Discovery* on p. 166 to each group. They should discuss and then report to the full class their conclusions.

6.   Students should continue their journaling with *Activity 5: Messages and Me* on p. 158 of the **ACTIVITY MANUAL**.

SKILL EVALUATION

I.   Skill Objectives 1-7:
      Students will improve their abilities to:
      1.   Use a wide variety of nonverbal communication forms to encode and decode meanings
      2.   Use facial and eye cues to receive and send information
      3.   Use spatial distance and markers to communicate intended meanings
      4.   Decode the possible meanings of artifacts and use artifacts to communicate their own meanings
      5.   Use touch cues to send and receive meaning
      6.   Use paralanguage to encode and decode intended meanings
      7.   Use silence signals to send and receive intended meanings

      A.   Ask students to individually demonstrate the following messages nonverbally. After their demonstration, they should be able to list the forms of nonverbal communication they used and justify their use.
            1.   You are about to meet with an employee to give them a superior performance rating.
            2.   You are about to meet with an employee to give them a poor

performance rating.

3.   Your child has just won first place in a track meet.
4.   Your child has just fallen and been disqualified from the track meet.
5.   You are late for a job interview. You want to indicate that it was unavoidable.

B.   Use the *Skill-Building Exercise: Expressing Feelings* on p. 146 as an evaluation tool.

C.   Use *Article 3: The Nonverbal Challenge Game* on p. 146 of the **ACTIVITY MANUAL** as an evaluation tool.

II.   Skill Objectives 8-9:
        Students will improve their abilities to:
        8.   Clarify informal time terms
        9.   Interpret time cues from a cultural perspective

Put students in pairs and ask them to act out a series of vignettes to cover a variety of formal and informal time terms, and cultural differences. Tape the vignettes for possible use in the future.

III.   Skill Objective 10: Students will improve their abilities to use nonverbal behaviors with an awareness of cultural differences and influences.

Provide a series of stimulus situations:
        a buyer in Japan
        a tourist in Latin America
        a social worker on a Navajo reservation
Put students in pairs and ask them to demonstrate some of the cultural differences in nonverbal communication in that situation.

Chapter 7
EMOTIONAL MESSAGES

CHAPTER OVERVIEW

Emotions involve our bodies, our minds, and cultural rules and beliefs. The most likely explanation for how emotions are aroused is that: an event occurs, we respond physiologically, we interpret this arousal, and we experience the emotion. There are several significant obstacles to effective communication of emotions. They include societal rules, fear of making oneself vulnerable, denial, and inadequate communication skills.

The following guidelines should help make emotional expression more meaningful: understand your feelings, decide if you wish to express your feelings, assess your communication options, describe your feelings as accurately as possible, identify the reasons for your feelings, anchor your feelings and their expression to the present time, and own your own feelings.

In responding to the emotions of others, try to see the situation from the perspective of the other person. Avoid focusing on yourself, show interest in the other person, and avoid evaluating the feelings of the other person.

Learning Objectives:

After completing this chapter, students should be able to:
1. Explain the nature of emotions and the role that the body, mind, and culture play
2. Explain how emotions are aroused and distinguish among emotions, emotional expressions, and emotional behavior
3. Identify and give examples of the major obstacles to effectively communicating emotions
4. Describe the guidelines for more effectively communicating and for responding to emotions

CLASSROOM APPROACHES

The Nature of Emotions (pp. 174-176)

Emphasis: Learning Objective 1
> Students will be able to explain the nature of emotions and the role that the body, mind, and culture play.

Emphasis: Skill Objective 1
> Students will improve their abilities to identify destructive and constructive beliefs about emotions and their communication.

Possible Methodologies:

1.   Lecture using the information on pp. 174-176. Use **Transparency Master 7-1**.

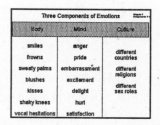

2.   Invite a doctor to speak to the class about the linkage between the body and emotions. What are some of the theories concerning the impact of emotion on health?

3.   Refer back to Chapter 6 on the nonverbal expression of emotions. Body language and affect displays demonstrate a relationship between emotions and their physical demonstration.

4.   Ask students to brainstorm a list of "good" emotions. Write their suggestions on a flipchart or chalk board. Then ask for a list of "bad" emotions. Write them so

that both lists can be seen.

Conduct a discussion on why some emotions are considered good and some are considered bad. Do any of the students disagree about emotions placed on one or the other of the lists? Does it make any difference when and where the emotions occur as to whether they are good or bad?

You may be able to develop a list of characteristics of "good" emotions and "bad" emotions from the ideas of the class.

What impact does culture have on which emotions are placed on which list?

5. Divide the class into small groups of 4-5 and ask each group to develop a scenario in which emotions would vary depending on interpretations. Include: the event, at least two different interpretations of the event (one should be positive, and one should be negative), the emotional reaction to each of the interpretations, and what the individual involved is likely to do as a result of each of the emotional reactions. Share the group results with the entire class.

6. Invite students or guests from different cultures to speak to the class about appropriate emotional expressions in their culture. You may be able to find ethnic social clubs (German, Greek, Italian, etc.) in your city, or people who work with Sister Cities, or businesses which regularly do business in other countries. Any of these would be good sources for speakers.

International business is such a priority now that there are a number of training programs on the market to teach people how to behave appropriately in other cultures. Businesses in your area may well be using or at least be aware of such programs which you could utilize.

Emotions and Emotional Arousal (pp. 177-183)

Emphasis: Learning Objective 2
Students will be able to explain how emotions are aroused and distinguish among emotions, emotional expression, and emotional behavior.

Emphasis: Skill Objective 2
Students will improve their ability to identify and communicate positive and negative emotions more appropriately

Possible Methodologies:

1. Lecture using the information on pp. 177-183 in **MESSAGES**. Use **Transparency Masters 7-2** and **7-3** for support.

2. Conduct a discussion on the cognitive-labeling theory of emotions. How does this theory impact one's perception of control over their emotions? How might you use this theory to help with such emotions as found in speech apprehension or stage fright? Use **Transparency Master 7-2** to guide the discussion.

    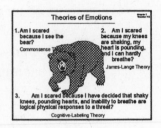

3. *Activity 1: Theories of Emotions* on p. 168 of the **ACTIVITY MANUAL** will allow students to apply information about theories of emotions.

4. Assign students to write a description of an emotional situation. At the conclusion, they should label the emotions, the emotional expressions, and the emotional behavior. **Transparency Master 7-3** can be of assistance to them.

    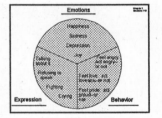

5. Show a portion of a film in class and ask students to identify the emotions, the emotional expressions, and the emotional behaviors. Possible films might include "Working Girl" (when the boss discovers the secretary has been playing her role), "Top Gun" (after the pilot is killed), "Rainman" (almost any scene with Dustin Hoffman has possibilities for discussion about incongruent emotions, expressions, and behaviors), "Bridges of Madison County" (as she is deciding whether to leave with him or not), or "While You Were Sleeping" (as she struggles with telling his family who she really is).

6. Place students in groups of 3-4 and assign one of the following scenarios to them:
    a. You are at a family gathering and learn that a family member has been killed on the way to join you.
    b. You are with your best friend. Both of you have recently been interviewed for a position with the same company. You receive word that you have been hired; your friend does not.
    c. Your mother is extremely worried about the trip you are planning to take to Europe with a group of friends.

d.   Your father disapproves of your decision to join the military after graduating from college.

Ask each group to discuss the emotions in the situation and decide how to appropriately communicate them. You might ask them to act out the situations both appropriately and inappropriately. Ask them to use the guidelines in the article, *Keeping Your Cool At Work,* on pp. 180-183 of **MESSAGES** as they plan how to react in each situation.

7.   Ask the students to take the *Self Test: How Do you Feel About Communicating Feelings?* on p. 179 of **MESSAGES**. In addition, have them analyze the situations described in item #5 above using the questions in the Self Test. What conclusions can they draw?

8.   Assign *Skill-Building Exercise 7.1: Expressing Negative Emotions* on pp. 185-186 of **MESSAGES** to develop skill in this area.

Obstacles in Communicating Emotions (pp. 183-186)

Emphasis: Learning Objective 3
Students will be able to identify and give examples of the major obstacles to effectively communicating emotions.

Emphasis: Skill Objective 3
Students will improve their abilities to combat the common obstacles for communicating emotions.

Possible Methodologies:
1.   Lecture using information on pp. 183-186.   Use **Transparency Masters 7-4** and **7-5** for support.

> "If you let your mind control your heart, you lose touch with the feelings that give life meaning."
>
> "The heart has its reasons which reason knows nothing of."
>
> Blaise Pascal

2.   Post three large flip chart pages around the room with one of the obstacles to effective emotional communication on each. Ask students to walk around to each of them and write examples on the pages. Then discuss one obstacle at a time, introducing it

with the examples written on the page. Use **Transparency Master 7-5**.

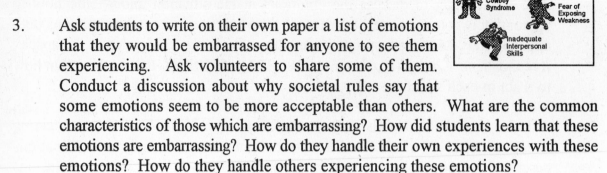

3. Ask students to write on their own paper a list of emotions that they would be embarrassed for anyone to see them experiencing. Ask volunteers to share some of them. Conduct a discussion about why societal rules say that some emotions seem to be more acceptable than others. What are the common characteristics of those which are embarrassing? How did students learn that these emotions are embarrassing? How do they handle their own experiences with these emotions? How do they handle others experiencing these emotions?

4. Collect Ann Landers columns with letters about a spouse or a friend who will not express or discuss emotions. Share these with the class as a stimulus for a discussion about how the inability to express emotions impacts relationships.

5. Assign students to interview a variety of people about their willingness to express emotions. Why (or why not) are they willing to do so? What is their greatest fear about expressing their honest emotions? What is their greatest hope? What was their greatest success in expressing emotions? What was their greatest failure?

6. Collect, or ask students to collect, sayings about the expression of emotions. Some examples include:

> "If you let your mind control your heart, you lose touch with the feelings that give life meaning."

> "The heart has its reasons which reason knows nothing of." Blaise Pascal (1623-1662)

> "Emotion has taught mankind (sic) to reason." Marquis de Vauvenargues (1715-1747)

> "All great discoveries are made by men (sic) whose feelings run ahead of their thinking." C. H. Parkhurst

Use **Transparency Master 7-4**: Feelings

---

7.   The benefits of expressing emotions are explored in *Activity 5: Confiding a Cure for Unemployment* on p. 181 of the **ACTIVITY MANUAL.**

Guidelines for Communicating Emotions (pp. 186-194)

Emphasis: Learning Objective 4
    Students will be able to describe the guidelines for more effectively communicating and for responding to emotions.

Emphasis: Skill Objective 4
    Students will improve their abilities to communicate emotions and respond to the emotions of others more effectively.

Possible Methodologies:

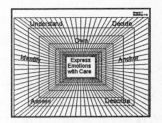

1.   Lecture using the information on pp. 186-194 in **MESSAGES**. Use **Transparency Masters 7-6** through **7-9** for support.

2.   Ask students to write a brief paragraph describing the most intense emotion they have felt. They do not need to share the content of the paragraph, but ask them to discuss whether it was easy or difficult to describe the emotion. What were limitations they may have felt? What may have made it easier? Have they ever described this particular emotion to anyone before? **Transparency Master 7-7** may help students describe their emotions.

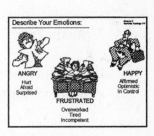

3.   Refer to *Skill-Building Exercise 7.2: Using The Language of Emotions* on pp. 188-189 of **MESSAGES** for practice in discussing emotions.

4.   Invite an actor to speak with the class about getting in touch with emotions needed in a play. How do actors do that? Have they developed a way of identifying, describing and feeling emotions? How do they use their bodies and their minds in putting an emotional portrayal together?

5.   Divide the class into groups of three. Ask the groups to allow each person to

describe a situation they feel comfortable sharing in which they have strong feelings. The other group members should help the individual understand his/her emotions, decide whether they wish to express their feelings, and then assess communication options. **Transparency Master 7-8** may be of assistance here.

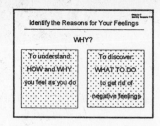

8.   *Skill-Building Exercise 7.3: Communicating Emotions Effectively* on p. 190-191 in **MESSAGES** is another opportunity for students to apply the guidelines for effective emotional communication.

9.   Divide students into groups of 6-7. Ask each group to develop a "Job Aid," a handy reference on effective emotional expression that a person could refer to when needed. Using the seven guidelines for emotional expression, the groups might make posters, business cards, songs, cheers, videos, audio tapes, or anything else which could be referred to in the future to remind them about effective emotional expression. Use **Transparency Master 7-6** for the seven guidelines.

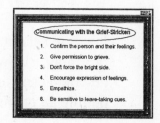

10.   Ask students to collect examples of people blaming their emotions on someone else. How frequently do they hear someone not "owning" their own emotions? Use **Transparency Master 7-9.**

11.   Invite someone from a Hospice program to speak to the class about communicating with the dying and/or their family.

12.   Give students who wish to an opportunity to share their own experiences with grieving. What were the best things people did and what were some of the worst?

13.   Use the information on *Communicating with the Grief-Stricken* on p. 193 of **MESSAGES** for practice in communicating with the grieving. Use **Transparency Master 7-10** for support.

14.   *Skill-Building Exercise 7.4, Responding to the Emotions of Others*, on pp. 193-194 of **MESSAGES** is an   o

---

pportunity to practice responding skills.

15. Invite a counselor to speak to the class about dealing with the emotions of others. What tips can be given from a counseling point of view?

16. Three activities of the **ACTIVITY MANUAL** deal with expressing emotions: *Activity 2: Expressing Emotions Responsibly* (p. 170), *Activity 3: Positive Emotions* (p. 174), and *Activity 4: A Few Calm Words about ANGER* (p. 176).

Critical Thinking

Possible Methodologies:

1. Divide the class into four groups. Assign each group one of the four suggestions for expressing emotions as found in the *Critical Thinking Sidebar* on p. 186 of **MESSAGES**. Each group should write three examples of how their suggestion could be used. They may share these with the class by a simple report or by acting them out.

2. Follow the same procedure as above, but assign each group one of the four suggestions against expressing emotions as found in the *Critical Thinking Sidebar* on p. 189 of **MESSAGES**. Each group should write three examples of how their suggestion could occur. They may share these with the class by a simple report or by acting them out.

3. Ask students to find examples of appeals to the emotions in magazines and newspapers. Assign them to analyze the effectiveness of the appeals. Use the *Critical Thinking Sidebar* on p. 191.

4. *Activity 6: Messages and Me* on p. 187 gives guidance as students write in their journals and their own feelings and emotions.

SKILL EVALUATION

I. Skill Objective 1: Identify destructive and constructive beliefs about emotions and their communication

Show a clip from a film such as "Private Benjamin" (showing a change in self image and/or a change in attitude toward the Army) or "Working Girl" (showing assumptions the characters have about each other) to allow students to identify constructive and destructive beliefs.

II.   Skill Objective 2: Identify and communicate positive and negative emotions more appropriately
   A.   Ask students to write a description of a situation which aroused strong emotions. Ask them to do a preliminary analysis on whether to express the emotions. Then they should write about how they would apply each of the suggestions for expressing emotions effectively.
   B.   An alternative to the suggestion above would be to have pairs of students prepare a demonstration of effective emotional expression. They should present it to the class as well as turn in a written explanation of why they expressed the emotions as they did.
   C.   *Activity 2: Expressing Emotions Responsibly and/or Activity 3: Positive Emotions* in the **ACTIVITY MANUAL** provide two other ways this Skill Objective could be evaluated.

III. Skill Objective 3: Combat the common obstacles for communicating emotions

   Use the situations in *Skill-Building Exercise 7.1: Expressing Negative Feelings* for students to identify specific obstacles which might be operating. How would they combat those obstacles in each instance?

IV.   Skill Objective 4: Communicate emotions and respond to the emotions of others more effectively

   A.   Set up a variety of situations for the students which would arouse strong emotions in them. They should then each write I-messages in response to each situation. You may wish to use the situations described in *Skill-Building Exercise 7.4* on p. 193 of **MESSAGES**.

   B.   Ask each student to write a scenario in which someone is experiencing grief. Then pair the students, let them explain their scenarios to each other, and then act out the way each of them would communicate.

Chapter 8
CONVERSATION MESSAGES

CHAPTER OVERVIEW:

Conversations usually follow a five step process: opening, feedforward, business, feedback, and closing.

Conversational management requires skill in the areas of initiating a conversation, maintaining a conversation, repairing a conversation, and closing it. There are two sets of skills for conversational effectiveness. First are four metaskills: mindfulness, flexibility, cultural sensitivity, and metacommunicational abilities. Then there are seven specific skills: openness, empathy, positiveness, immediacy, interaction management, expressiveness, and other-orientation.

Learning Objectives

After completing this chapter, students should be able to:
1.   Explain the five-step model of conversation
2.   Explain the processes involved in opening, maintaining, and closing conversations
3.   Explain the skills for conversational effectiveness

Skill Objectives

After completing this chapter, students should improve their abilities to:
1.   Follow the basic structure for conversation
2.   Initiate, maintain, and close conversations more effectively
3.   Use the principles of conversational effectiveness (openness, empathy, positiveness, immediacy, interaction management, expressiveness, and other-orientation) with mindfulness, flexibility, cultural sensitivity, and metacommunication

CLASSROOM APPROACHES

The Conversation Process (pp. 202-210)

Emphasis: Learning Objective 1
  Students will be able to explain the five-step model of conversation.

Emphasis: Skill Objective 1
  Students will improve their ability to follow the basic structure for conversation.

Possible Methodologies:

1. Lecture using the information on pp. 202-210 of **MESSAGES**. Use **Transparency Masters 8-1** and **8-2**.

 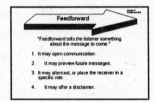

2. Administer the *Self Test: How Satisfactory Is Your Conversation?* on pp. 200-202 of **MESSAGES**. Ask students to identify the characteristics of conversation which are most important to them personally.

3. To introduce ways we typically open conversations, tape record the students as they arrive at class. Play the tape for the class to demonstrate the varieties of interaction and the ways people signal their willingness to communicate.

4. Bring to class a collection of introductory materials: the preface to a book, a table of contents, movie blurbs, magazine covers, speech introductions, the first paragraph of a newspaper story, etc. Ask students to examine them and identify what particular purpose each is designed for. Compare these purposes to the purposes of feedforward.

5. Tell several "good news, bad news" jokes to illustrate feedforward used to preview future messages.

6.	Explain that you don't want to seem disorganized, but that you do want students to turn back to Chapter 1 to review about relational messages. Ask students to give other examples of classic disclaimers. Use **Transparency Master 8-3** to assist in discussing the five types of disclaimers as well as *Table 8.1: Conversational Disclaimers* on p. 204 of **MESSAGES.**

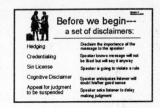

7.	Use *Activity 2: Categorizing Disclaimers* on p. 200 of the **ACTIVITY MANUAL** for practice in identifying types of disclaimers.

8.	Assign students to make notes on three conversations they have in the next day. Identify the steps of the model in each conversation. Did the conversations follow the model clearly? Were steps distinct, or were some steps combined?

9.	Ask students to listen for conversations in which some of the steps are ineffective or inappropriate. How could the step have been improved?

10.	Think of people with whom you feel uncomfortable. Are inappropriate conversational skills a contributing factor to your discomfort? How might you assist the individual in improving conversational skills?

 11.	Have students encountered cultural differences in conversational style? Ask for examples. Use *Table 8.2: Conversational Taboos Around the World* on p. 207 of **MESSAGES** to stimulate discussion.

Conversational Management (pp. 210-218)

Emphasis: Learning Objective 2
	Students will be able to explain the processes involved in opening, maintaining, and closing conversations.

Emphasis: Skill Objective 2
	Students will improve their abilities to initiate, maintain, and close conversations more effectively

Possible Methodologies:

1.   Lecture using information on pp. 210-218 of **MESSAGES**. **Transparency Masters 8-4** through **8-7** support this information.

2.   Place students in groups of 4. Assign each group 2 or 3 of the conversationally difficult people on pp. 211-212 of **MESSAGES**. Ask the groups to develop a brief skit illustrating each.

3.   Ask students to listen for examples of conversationally difficult people. How do they feel about those people? How do they typically behave when confronted by one of them?

4.   After discussing the text material on opening conversations, assign the following situations to pairs of students. Ask them to plan how they would handle the situation and then to role play it for the class. Use **Transparency Master 8-4** to assist the students as they plan their role plays.

a.   You and another student arrive at the same time for the first day of class and are there alone.

b.   You arrive at a party. Several other people are there, but you do not know any of them. Your friend, the host, is busy in another room.

c.   You are in a new job. Everyone else seems to know each other.

d.   You are in the college cafeteria eating alone when you notice another person, also alone, whom you have seen in your English Literature class. The two of you have never spoken before.

Divide students into groups of about 3-4. Each group should plan additional situations in which someone needs to open a conversation. Pair two groups together; each one will role-play the other group's situation. Discuss the approach used and how successful it would be likely to be.

5.   Students should listen to conversations over the next day. Make note of how many are initiated by self-references, other references, relational references, or context references. How many of the conversations did they themselves initiate? Which kind of reference feels most comfortable? Do different circumstances and/or different people make different kinds of openings feel more or less comfortable?

6. Put students in small groups and ask them to brainstorm as many different "opening lines" as they can think of. Then assess the lines: which ones would they actually use? Which ones would they respond positively to? Are there differences in the reactions of the male students as opposed to the female students?

7. Play a segment from a movie such as *Apollo 13, First Knight, Fried Green Tomatoes,* or *True Lies*. Ask students to identify examples of speaker cues and listener cues. Use **Transparency Master 8-5** for support.

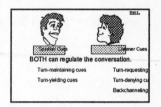

6. Assign an experiment. Ask students to deliberately use only positive listening cues in three conversations, and then to use only negative listener cues in another three conversations. Make notes on the reactions of the speakers. A variation of this experiment might be to have students see how long they can keep a speaker speaking through positive and reinforcing listener cues.

7. Set up a contest for students to see who can collect the highest number of actual excuses heard in the course of a specified period of time. What are the conversational problems which lead to the speaker's need for an excuse? You may wish to subdivide the contest so there can be a winner in each of the types of excuses (as listed in *Skill-Building Exercise 8.2: Formulating Excuses* on p. 217 of **MESSAGES**). Use **Transparency Master 8-6.**

8. Ask students to interview professors to find out what kinds of excuses students tend to use. Which ones are the most effective? Why?

9. Pay attention to closings used in telephone conversations. Ask students to bring in examples. Do they note differences in the ways people close conversations on the telephone as opposed to those in person? Use **Transparency Master 8-7**

10. Have students take a poll of 10 of their friends. They should ask: "How do I usually end a conversation with you?" Discuss their findings in class.

Conversational Effectiveness (pp. 218-230)

Emphasis: Learning Objective 3
Students will be able to explain the skills for conversational effectiveness.

Emphasis: Skill Objective 3
Students will improve their abilities to use the principles of conversational effectiveness (openness, empathy, positiveness, immediacy, interaction management, expressiveness, and other orientation) with mindfulness, flexibility, cultural sensitivity, and metacommunication.

Possible Methodologies:

1. Lecture using the information on pp. 218-230 of **MESSAGES**. **Transparency Masters 8-8** and **8-9** relate to this section.

2. Have students take the *Self-Test: How Flexible Are You in Communication?* on p. 219 of **MESSAGES**. How sensitive do they find themselves to be? Place them in groups of 3 and ask them to develop both a positive and a negative application of each of the statements in the assessment.

3. Assign students to practice metacommunication by choosing a good friend and asking him/her to help with the assignment. Discuss the kinds of conversations the students and friends usually have: how mindful of communication skills/rules are they? how flexible are they? how sensitive to cultural differences are they? how often do they talk about their communication? how might they improve their conversations? Use **Transparency Master 8-8** to guide your discussion.

4. The book, **The Outer Bank**, by Anne Rivers Siddons has numerous examples of effective and ineffective conversational styles. Ask students to look for rules which are deliberately broken, for lack of sensitivity, and for metacommunication examples. Any of Pat Conroy's books also provide excellent examples of communication styles. Consider **Beach Music**, **The Great Santini**, or **Prince of Tides**.

5.   Use *Tips for Teasers - and Targets* on pp. 223-224 of **MESSAGES**. Ask students to talk to friends to collect examples of times when teasing was fun and times when teasing was not fun.

6.   Use **Transparency Master 8-9** to introduce each element of conversational effectiveness.

7.   Demonstrate openness by using open-ended questions to keep a conversation flowing:

   a.   Divide the students into pairs. Ask them to choose a well-known person to interview and then to plan five open-ended questions to ask the person.

   b.   Divide students into groups of 7-10. Ask them to plan and present a skit showing the difference between a conversation based on open-ended questions and one based on closed questions.

8.   Practice expressing empathy:

   a.   After assigning students to read the section in the text on learning empathy, ask them to write about their own childhood. They should describe an incident in which they learned empathy, or saw and/or felt empathy.

   b.   In general class discussion or in small groups, ask students to describe situations which require empathy. Ask them to consider the impact of showing sympathy instead.

   c.   Place students in small groups and ask them to develop a skit in which empathy is required. They are to demonstrate the suggestions listed on p. 225-226 of **MESSAGES**. A variation would be to ask half the groups to give positive examples and half the groups to give negative examples of expressing empathy.

9.   *Activity 3: You Just Don't Understand* on p. 202 of the **ACTIVITY MANUAL** gives students an opportunity to explore gender differences in conversations.

10. Demonstrate positiveness by writing a brief note for each member of the class expressing your appreciation for them. Try to name some specific behavior you particularly like. As people arrive in class, give them their notes. After they have had a chance to read them, discuss how it feels to receive positive strokes. Were they surprised? Were any of the comments about behaviors no one had ever

complimented before? Are they more or less likely to continue behavior which has been complimented? How might they pass on positive strokes to someone else?

11.   Use *Activity 1: Compliments: Verbal Gifts* on p. 196 of the **ACTIVITY MANUAL** to give students some skill practice on positiveness.

12.   Use **Transparency Master 8-10** to explain immediacy. 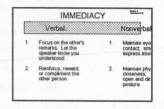 Practice immediacy by asking students to spend the following day making a concentrated effort to demonstrate immediacy; reinforce, reward, or compliment others; and focus on the remarks of others. Ask them to make notes about the reactions of the other people. At the next class meeting, discuss the reactions they encountered. What are some commonalities among the reactions? Did anyone receive comments about their behavior? How did the students feel about trying these behaviors? What conclusions do they draw about the impact of immediacy on interpersonal communication?

13.   Assess levels of interaction management:
      a.   Use the *Self-Test: Are You a High Self-Monitor?* on pp. 227-228 of **MESSAGES**. Ask students to assess how accurate their results feel.
      b.   Ask the class to list situations which require a fairly high level of self-monitoring. How comfortable do they feel in such situations?

14.   Practice expressiveness in interactions:
      a.   Ask the class for examples of how the concept of expressiveness is similar to that of openness.
      b.   Research shows that expressive individuals are considered more credible than those who aren't. Ask students to think of a public speaker they particularly like to listen to: how expressive is that person? in what ways is the person expressive -- verbally and nonverbally?
      c.   Ask students to enlist a family member to give them some feedback on when they are most expressive and involved, and when they are not.

15.   Practice an other-orientation:
      Give the class an assignment to apply the ideas of other-orientation for a 24-hour period. In each of their interactions, they should attempt to spend more time listening to others than in speaking. An exercise to assist their focus on the other

person is to periodically paraphrase what the other person has said.

16.   Review conversational skills:
John T. Malloy's book, <u>Malloy's Live for</u> <u>Success</u>, by Bantam Books, 1981, is an excellent resource for discussion of the use of verbal and nonverbal conversational skills in interactions.

17.   Read *Activity 4: The Sounds of Silence, How to Talk Your Way to a Better Marriage* on p. 206 of the **ACTIVITY MANUAL** as a way of reviewing principles of effective conversations.

 Critical Thinking Skills

Possible Methodologies:

1.   Use *Critical Thinking Sidebar: Applying the Feedback Model to Relationships* on p. 208 of **MESSAGES**. Continue to work with the idea of applying concepts from one area to another area in the following way: List concepts or topics from this chapter on separate small pieces of paper. Have each student draw one slip of paper. Pair them randomly and ask the students to come up with some way that their two concepts relate. To stretch this exercise, mix concepts from more than one chapter, or from a chapter and from another book.

2.   Consider the kinds of metaskills which help you conduct yourself effectively in a conversation. *Critical Thinking Sidebar: Metaskills* on p. 218 of **MESSAGES** will be helpful. John Malloy's **Live for Success** provides an example of a man who was ineffective in conversations. What metaskills did he lack? Ask students to identify people who are skilled in conversation and those who are not. Through observation, students should identify several specific metaskills.

3.   Divide students into six groups. Assign each group one of the questions in the *Critical Thinking Sidebar: Discovery* on p. 230 of **MESSAGES**. Ask them to discuss and report back to the class.

4.   *Activity 5: Messages and Me* on p. 210 of the **ACTIVITY MANUAL** will give students ideas for their journal entries related to this chapter.

SKILL EVALUATION

I.   **Skill Objective 1:** Follow the basic structure for conversation

Play a videotaped segment of a conversation in a movie. Students must assess and identify each of the conversational steps in the taped segment, and then, in pairs, plan and present an improved version of the conversation.

II.   **Skill Objective 2:** Initiate, maintain, and close conversations more effectively

    A.   Assign students to groups of three. Their task is to go out on campus and let each member of the group open a conversation with a stranger. One of the other members should take notes identifying the strategies used; the third will assess the effectiveness of the strategy and determine a grade. (If a video camera is available, let students videotape themselves.)

    B.   Continue the exercise above on opening a conversation to allow the interacting group member to close the conversation. Once again, one group member should take notes about what happened; the other group member will analyze the effectiveness of the strategy and determine a grade.

III.   **Skill Objective 3:** Use the principles of conversational effectiveness (openness, empathy, positiveness, immediacy, interaction management, expressiveness, and other-orientation) with mindfulness, flexibility, cultural sensitivity, and metacommunication

Each pair of students should plan an interaction which will allow them to demonstrate all seven qualities for interpersonal effectiveness. They must then present their interaction to the rest of the class which will be assigned to identify each of the qualities as they are demonstrated.

Chapter 9
INTERPERSONAL COMMUNICATION AND CULTURE

CHAPTER OVERVIEW:

Travel, political and economic changes, communication technology and changing immigration patterns have all made intercultural communication more significant in our lives than ever before.

Culture consists of the values, beliefs, behavior, artifacts and communication of a group of people. It is their specialized life-style. In particular, it impacts communication and behavior between cultures, races, ethnic groups, religions and nations.

Cultures differ in a number of ways. Orientations may be individualistic or collectivist; information may be found in the context in high-context cultures or explicitly in the message in low-context cultures; and messages are sent and received according to rules and customs which vary among cultures.

The term "intercultural communication" may refer to interactions of several kinds: between cultures, between races, between ethnic groups, between religions, and between nations.

There are many barriers to intercultural communication. We stereotype, we ignore differences between ourselves and those who are different, we ignore differences in verbal and nonverbal messages, we violate cultural rules and customs, we react negatively to cultural differences. We can, however, avoid intercultural barriers by recognizing the differences between ourselves and others, recognizing the differences which exist among group members, being aware of cultural rules, and avoiding negative evaluations. In addition, we can remember that meanings are in people, not in words or gestures.

Finally, we may enhance intercultural communication by utilizing the principles for effective conversation in our intercultural interactions: openness, empathy, positiveness, immediacy, interaction management, expressiveness, and other-orientation.

Learning Objectives

After completing this chapter, students should be able to:
1. Explain why intercultural communication is so important today
2. Define *intercultural communication* and explain the model of intercultural communication
3. Explain the how ethnocentrism, mindlessness, and fear may pose difficulties in studying intercultural communication
4. Describe at least five barriers to intercultural communication
5. Explain how the characteristics of conversational effectiveness apply to intercultural communication

Skill Objectives

After completing this chapter, students should improve their abilities to:
1. Send and receive intercultural communication in light of high and low context differences
2. Communicate with the recognition that meanings are largely culturally determined
3. Identify potential problems in intercultural communication
4. Avoid the common barriers to intercultural communication
5. Use the principles of interpersonal effectiveness as appropriate

CLASSROOM APPROACHES

Importance of Intercultural Communication (pp. 239-241; 245-248)

Emphasis: Learning Objective 1

Students will be able to explain why intercultural communication is so important today.

Emphasis: Skill Objective 1

Students will improve their abilities to send and receive intercultural communication in light of high and low context differences.

Possible Methodologies:

1.   Lecture using information on pp. 239-241; 245-248 of
      MESSAGES.   Use **Transparency Master 9-1** to
      reinforce ideas in this section.

2.   Invite a guest speaker from a business which does
      extensive work in other cultures. Someone from Pier
      One, Tandy/Radio Shack, Bombay Company, or almost any other large business
      will have individuals with experience in learning other cultures. Ask them to talk
      about why their company is involved internationally, what barriers and difficulties
      they have encountered, and why it is worth the effort to learn to communicate
      cross culturally.

3.   Invite members of the international students' organization on your campus to visit
      in your class. Have them discuss why they are studying in the United States. Ask
      if any members of the class have studied abroad and have them share their
      experiences.

4.   Ask students to read *Activity 1: Culture Shock* on p. 218 of the **ACTIVITY
      MANUAL**. Ask them to use the three stages described to analyze an experience
      of their own with some form of different culture.

5.   See if your campus or a local business has videoconferencing equipment you could
      use to speak to someone in another country. This technology allows two-way
      interactive video and is an exciting demonstration of the impact that technology
      has on communication in general and on access to international and cross cultural
      communication.

      Kinko's has videoconferencing equipment available in many of their stores. You
      may wish to purchase some time on their equipment or ask if they would be willing
      to provide a demonstration.

      If the equipment is not readily available, perhaps someone who uses
      videoconferencing could speak to the class. Vendors will be glad to provide you
      with videotapes demonstrating the technology so that students can get a feel for the
      impact it is having. AT&T may be willing to demonstrate their new video phone.

In addition to videoconferencing, you may want to explore satellite transmissions and audioconferencing. An organization such as the International Teleconferencing Association may be able to help you set up an audioconference for your class.

6.   *Activity 2: Personal Culture Diagram* on p. 222 of the **ACTIVITY MANUAL** will help students assess their own cultural background and how it may impact the way they interpret the rest of the chapter as well as many of their intercultural interactions.

7.   Ask students to identify examples of individualistic and collectivist cultures: in the context of political systems, schools, clubs and organizations, sports, and religions. Do they find themselves participating in some of each? Or are they primarily in one type of culture or the other? Look at *Table 9.1: Individual and Collective Culture Differences*. With which list of characteristics are your most comfortable personally?

8.   Ask students to identify a specific example of a high-context and a low-context culture. They should then write an example of the same communication situation within the two cultures and how it would be handled.

The Nature of Intercultural Communication (pp. 241-251)

Emphasis: Learning Objective 2
Students will be able to define *intercultural communication* and explain the model of intercultural communication.

Emphasis: Skill Objective 2
Students will improve their abilities to communicate with the recognition that meanings are largely culturally determined.

Possible Methodologies:
1.   Lecture using the information on pp. 241-251 of **MESSAGES**. **Transparency Masters 9-2** and **9-3** relate to this material.

2.   Before you assign the chapter to be read, begin a class by reading the story of the Nacirema to the class. Preface it by asking the class to take note of unusual cultural practices in the story. When you finish, ask the class to contrast the Nacirema with other cultures they know. Eventually discuss how many immediately recognized that the story was about Americans and how many did not. Why was the story recognizable and why was it not?

3.   Assign a writing task. Students should select a group with which they are very familiar (a sorority or fraternity, a denomination, a school, a club, a group of friends, etc.) and write a description of them following the model of the story of the Nacirema. They are to pretend they have never encountered this group before; how would their cultural practices appear? How would they be described? When the students turn in their papers, ask several to volunteer to read theirs. See if the class can identify the group being described.

4.   This assignment is similar to the one above in that the students should select a group with which they are very familiar but which once was new to them. This time, ask them to write about how they learned the cultural practices of the group. Was anything strange at first? How does it seem now? Have they been involved in passing the culture on to others? How does that feel?

5.   Place students in groups of 3-5. Ask them to brainstorm all the different cultures which they represent. How many do they share? Discuss the cultures which are unique to one person in the group. Contrast how that culture is perceived by the person within it and those who are not a part of it.

6.   After students read the article, "Corporate Culture: How Not To Get Sucked In," on pp. 248-251 of **MESSAGES**, ask them to follow *Activity 3: Corporate Culture* on p. 225 of the **ACTIVITY MANUAL**.

Difficulties in Studying Intercultural Communication (pp. 241 - 244)

Emphasis: Learning Objective 3

>Students will be able to explain the how ethnocentrism, mindlessness, and fear may pose difficulties in studying intercultural communication.

Emphasis: Skill Objective 3

>Students will improve their abilities to identify potential problems in intercultural communication.

Possible Methodologies:

1. Lecture using the information on pp. 251-254 of **MESSAGES**. **Transparency Master 9-4** will be helpful.

2. A good example of ethnocentrism is found is the article *Case Study of a Nonconscious Ideology: Training the Woman to Know Her Place* by Sandra L. Bem and Daryl J. Bem in the book **Beliefs, Attitudes, and Human Affairs** by Daryl Bem (Brooks-Cole Publishing Company, 1970). They argue that nonconscious beliefs about women motivate a host of subtle practices that people would not support if they were able to consciously think about what they are doing. An excellent statement illustrating the tendency to see things through our own filters is the following: "Only a very unparochial and intellectual fish is aware that his (sic) environment is wet. After all, what else could it be? Such is the nature of a nonconscious ideology." (p. 89)

3. Ask students to work in groups of 3-4 using *Table 9.2: The Ethnocentrism Continuum* on p. 253 of **MESSAGES**. Using their school, they are to identify a group within the school for each of the degrees of ethnocentrism listed. They are then to list specific communications behaviors which illustrate the differences among the levels of ethnocentrism.

4. *Activity 4: Words and Culture*, on p. 226 of the **ACTIVITY MANUAL** gives students a chance to see how language can function to reinforce ethnocentrism. Do they use any of these words? Are they offended by any of these words?

5. Ask students to provide personal examples of operating in a mindless state. How have they become mindful of that?

6.   Let students take the *Self-Test: How Open Are You Interculturally?* on pp. 244-245 of **MESSAGES**. In what ways might they identify areas where they experience fear?

Obstacles to Intercultural Communication (pp. 244 - 250)

Emphasis: Learning Objective 4
   Students will be able to describe at least five barriers to intercultural communication.

Emphasis: Skill Objective 2
   Students will improve their abilities to avoid the common barriers to intercultural communication.

Possible Methodologies:
1.   Lecture using the information on pp. 244 - 250 of **MESSAGES**. **Transparency Masters 9-5** through **9-9** illustrate the various barriers.

2.   Use *Skill Building Exercise 9.1: Dealing with Intercultural Problems* on p. 255 in **MESSAGES**.

3.   A model for learning culture and avoiding barriers is provided in *Learning Intercultural Communication Competence* by Linda Beamer in **The Journal of Business Communication**, Volume 29, Number 3, 1992. It includes the following steps: acknowledging diversity, organizing information according to stereotypes, posing questions to challenge the stereotypes, analyzing communication episodes, and generating "other culture" messages. (The entire issue of the journal is devoted to intercultural communication.)

4.   An excellent resource for learning about different cultures and the potential problems an American might have in learning them is found in a newsletter called **CULTURGRAMS**. Each four-page newsletter provides information for one of about 100 countries on customs and courtesies, the people, lifestyle, the nation, and references for additional study. For information on **CULTURGRAMS** and other resources, write to the Publication Services, David M. Kennedy Center for

International Studies, 280 HRCB, Brigham Young University, Provo, Utah, 84602.

5. Chapter 6 on nonverbal communication refers to a series of books by Roger E. Axtell on gestures. They are referenced here again because of their significance cross-culturally. The books, all from John Wiley & Sons, Inc. are:

Gestures: The Do's and Taboos of Body Language Around the World
Do's and Taboos Around the World
The Do's and Taboos of International Trade: A Small Business Primer
Do's and Taboos of Hosting International Visitors

6. Invite a trainer from a business which sends executives to other countries. Ask them to demonstrate to your class some of the training they do for their company.

7. Consider using a cross-cultural simulation such as **Bafa-Bafa. Simsoc** is another simulation which allows students to feels some of the impact of cultural differences and barriers. If you do use a simulation, be sure to schedule sufficient time to debrief the experience. Its value to the students is in their reflection on their own behaviors and reactions during the simulation.

8. Discuss each of the obstacles identified. Use **Transparency Masters 9-5 - 9-9**.

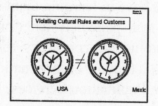

9.   Use *Skill Building Exercise 9.2: Explaining Cultural Rules and Differences* on pp. 257-258 of **MESSAGES** as a way to review all the possible obstacles to intercultural communication.

10.   Some specific ways to help students avoid treating differences negatively when they encounter people with disabilities are listed on p. 259 of **MESSAGES** in *Table 9.3: Ten Commandments for Communicating with People with Disabilities.*

11.   Language differences are a special category of cultural differences. Read the article in *Activity 5: Specialist in Women and Other Diseases* on p. 230 of the **ACTIVITY MANUAL** for some humorous examples.

Gateways to Intercultural Communication (pp. 260-264)

Emphasis: Learning Objective 5
       Students will be able to explain how the characteristics of conversational effectiveness apply to intercultural communication.

Emphasis: Skill Objective 5
       Students will improve their abilities to use the principles of interpersonal effectiveness as appropriate.

Possible Methodologies:
1.   Lecture using the information on pp. 260-264 of **MESSAGES**. **Transparency Masters 9-10** and **8-9** will be helpful. (Note that **Transparency Master 8-9** is found in Chapter 8.)

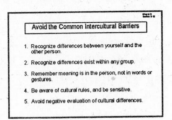

2.   As either introduction or conclusion to this section of the chapter, use *Skill-*

Building Exercise 9.4: Confronting Intercultural Difficulties on p. 263 of **MESSAGES**.

3.   Send students to interview someone from a different culture. They are to keep a journal identifying potential barriers and the specific conversational principle they used to overcome the barrier.

Critical Thinking

Possible Methodologies:

1.   Analysis and synthesis are important processes for understanding a communication event fully. Read *Critical Thinking Sidebar: Analysis* on p. 241 and *Critical Thinking Sidebar: Synthesis* on p. 242 of **MESSAGES**. Ask students to use both these processes to discuss a communication experience they have had with someone from a different culture.

2.   This chapter discusses the contrast between high and low-context cultures. *Critical Thinking Sidebar: Appreciating the Middle* on p. 246 of **MESSAGES** will help students assess cultures which are at neither extreme.

3.   Assign students to read the newspaper and listen to several popular radio talk show hosts. They are to identify appeals made to fear concerning a given cultural group and collect them to share with the class. *Critical Thinking Sidebar: Fear Appeals* on p. 253 of **MESSAGES** will be helpful.

4.   Place students in groups of 4-5 and ask them to discuss the questions in *Critical Thinking Sidebar: Discovery* on p. 264 of **MESSAGES**. Ask the groups to share and discuss their ideas with the other groups.

5.   Students should use *Activity 6: Messages and Me* on p. 232 of the **ACTIVITY MANUAL** to continue their critical thinking through journaling.

SKILL EVALUATION

I.   Skill Objective 1: Send and receive intercultural communications in light of high and low context differences

Ask students to identify as many types of intercultural communication as they can within this class, within the college, within the university, within the community. Then ask if they can identify a situation in which there would be NO intercultural communication at all because everyone shares the same culture. Which of the types identified are high context and which are low context? Ask students to choose two of their examples of high context and two of their examples of low context and plan a message for each.

II.   Skill Objective 2: Communicate with the recognition that meanings are largely culturally determined.

Use *Skill-Building Exercise 9.2: Explaining Cultural Rules and Differences* on pp. 257-258 of **MESSAGES.** In pairs, the students should act out ways the participants could adapt their own cultures in order to communicate more effectively with the other.

III.   Skill Objective 3: Identify potential problems in intercultural communication.

     A.   Show a segment of a Japanese film. Ask students to identify how the five barriers to intercultural communication could make it difficult for them to understand the film.

     B.   *Skill-Building Exercise 9.1: Dealing with Intercultural Problems* on p. 255 of **MESSAGES** can be used as an evaluation tool.

IV.   Skill Objective 4: Avoid the common barriers to intercultural communication.

Use *Skill-Building Exercise 9.4: Confronting Intercultural Difficulties* as an evaluation tool. Place students in pairs and ask them to demonstrate the ways they would avoid common barriers in these situations.

V.   Skill Objective 5: Use the principles of interpersonal effectiveness as appropriate.

Skill-Building Exercise 9.3: Random Pairs on p. 261 of **MESSAGES** makes an excellent evaluation tool for students to demonstrate the principles of interpersonal effectiveness. Have students draw numbers to assign them their situations and then ask them to demonstrate effective communication behavior.

Chapter 10
INTERPERSONAL COMMUNICATION
AND RELATIONSHIPS

CHAPTER OVERVIEW:

People are drawn to develop interpersonal relationships for several reasons, among them to alleviate loneliness, to gain stimulation, to gain self-knowledge, to increase self-esteem, and to maximize pleasure and minimize pain. Relationships develop along fairly predictable patterns, from contact to involvement, intimacy, deterioration, repair and dissolution, but they may stop at any given stage or go forward or backwards.

We are attracted to other people because of at least four factors: attractiveness, proximity, reinforcement, and similarity.

There are four theories to explain what happens when we develop, maintain, and dissolve interpersonal relationships. These theories are: attraction, social penetration, social exchange, and equity.

Learning Objectives

After completing this chapter, students should be able to:

1. Identify and explain at least four reasons for relationship development
2. Explain the six-stage model of interpersonal relationships
3. Explain attraction, rules, social penetration, social exchange, and equity theories
4. Explain the suggestions for improving communication in relationships

---

Skill Objectives

After completing this chapter, students should improve their abilities to:
1. Formulate both verbal and nonverbal messages appropriate to their relationship stage
2. Assess their own relationships in terms of attraction, rules, social penetration, social exchange, and equity theories
3. Use empathy and self-disclosures, be open to change, fight fair, and be reasonable in relationship communication

CLASSROOM APPROACHES

Relationship Stages (pp. 270-292)

Emphasis: Learning Objectives 1 and 2
   Students will be able to:
   1. identify and explain at least four reasons for relationship development.
   2. Explain the six-stage model of interpersonal relationships

Emphasis: Skill Objective 1
   Students will improve their abilities to formulate both verbal and nonverbal messages appropriate to their relationship stage

Possible Methodologies:
1. Lecture using information on pp. 270-292 of **MESSAGES**. Use **Transparency Master** 10-1 and 10-2 for support.

2. Post five signs around the room, each with one of the reasons for the development of relationships written on it. Ask students to group around one that they are willing to share some experience with. The students at that sign should then tell of their own experiences with that reason for developing a relationship.

3. Divide students into five groups. Assign one of the reasons for relationships to

roles. Then ask them to give reasons relationships may fail to fill these roles. Use **Transparency Master 10-1** to guide the discussion.

4. Have students write an essay about friendship. They may wish to focus on their best friend, on what friendship means to them, on the pros and cons of their current friendships, or on the role they feel they play in their friendships with others. **Transparency Master 10-2** may give them some ideas as they write.

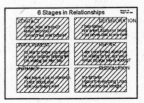

5. Put students in pairs. Assign one of the six stages of a relationship to each of the pairs. Their task is to plan and act out a short skit demonstrating their stage. Use **Transparency Master 10-3** for reference.

6. Show a movie or a television program which would allow students to identify the six stages of relationships. They may want to use Table 10.1 on pp. 272 of **MESSAGES** as a reference.

7. *Activity 3: What TYPE Are You?* of the **ACTIVITY MANUAL** will help students understand why they encounter differences in the ways people experience the stages in relationships. You may wish to invite a counselor who uses the **Myers-Briggs Type Indicator** to help the class understand their scores and the applications of the MBTI information. The counseling office at your school may well use the MBTI, particularly to assist students as they make career choices. This would be an excellent tool for students to know about.

The Myers-Briggs Type Indicator is one of the most extensively used personality assessment instruments for non-psychiatric populations. It is often used in marriage counseling and with work groups to help them improve their relationships. Give the class time to do the brief version of the instrument and then discuss the "types" they are. Are their best friends in the class the same type or different?

The source for the Myers-Briggs Type Indicator is referenced in Chapter 3. **Type Talk** is referenced in the **ACTIVITY MANUAL**. Additional books on the Myers-Briggs are:

Bates, Marilyn and Keirsey, David W., **Please Understand Me**. Del Mar, Calif.: Prometheus Nemesis Book Company, 1978.

Lawrence, Gordon, **People Types and Tiger Stripes**. Gainesville, Fla.: Center for Application of Psychological Type, Inc., 1982. (This book focuses on the use of the Myers-Briggs in education and has many helpful ideas on the development of teaching and learning strategies for teachers and students of various types.)

Myers, Isabel Briggs, **Gifts Differing**. Palo Alto, Calif.: Consulting Psychologists Press, 1985.

Isachsen, Olaf, and Berens, Linda V., **Working Together: A Personality Centered Approach to Management**. Coronado, CA: Neworld Management Press, 1988.

8. Invite a marriage counselor to speak to the class about the six stages and/or the six love styles. What advice might be given to avoid deterioration and dissolution? What needs to happen at the other stages to keep a relationship healthy? What are some of the strategies they suggest for relationship repair?

9. Ask students to write a brief paragraph describing their philosophy of love. Then ask them to take the *Test Yourself: What Kind of Lover Are You?* on pp. 278-281 of **MESSAGES**. Do their descriptions match the test results? Discuss what happens when people with different philosophies of love enter into a relationship. **Transparency Master 10-4** highlights the kinds of love identified in the test.

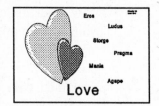

10. Ask students individually to think of a relationship they would like to reinforce or change in some way, or repair. Assign them to write an analysis which describes the stages the relationship has gone through, the stage it is currently in, and where they want the relationship to go. Then have them write a contract for themselves describing behavior and/or language they will use to accomplish moving the relationship in their desired direction. **Transparency Master 10-5** outlines steps for general relationship repair.

11. Ask students to practice asking for positive behaviors from those with whom they are in a relationship. Reference *Skill-Building Exercise 10.2: Asking for Positive Behaviors* on pp. 282-284 of **MESSAGES**.

12. Develop role-play situations requiring disengagement strategies for the students to plan and act out. I suggest a behavior-modeling process in which one student acts as the disengager, one as the disengagee, one as an observer, and one as a coach. After the role-play is complete and fully discussed by the coach and observer, the four students should switch roles and do a new role-play. Follow this procedure until all students have had a chance to play all roles. Use *Skill-Building Exercise 10.3: Using Disengagement Strategies* on p. 288 of **MESSAGES** to give the students guidance.

13. *Activity 4: More Typewatching -- Procrastinating, Fighting, and Loving* on p. 256 of the **ACTIVITY MANUAL** provides additional insight as students work through a deteriorating relationship or as they seek to maintain a good one.

Theories of Relational Development (pp. 292-300)

Emphasis: Learning Objective 3
Students will be able to explain attraction, rules, social penetration, social exchange, and equity theories.

Emphasis: Skill Objective 2
Students will improve their abilities to assess their own relationships in terms of attraction, rules, social penetration, social exchange, and equity theories.

Possible Methodologies:
1. Lecture using information on pp. 292-300 of **MESSAGES**. Use **Transparency Masters 10-6** through **10-10** for support.

2. Ask students to individually write down the names of their three best friends. Then ask them to write beside each name what originally attracted them to that person. Discuss some of the student's lists.

Review the four factors on pp. 292-294 of **MESSAGES** and compare them to the reasons listed by the students.

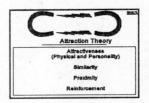

3. Ask students to make four columns on a piece of paper. Head each column with one of the four factors leading to interpersonal attraction. Then ask students to list the names of friends in the appropriate column who are attractive to them because of that factor. Use **Transparency Masters 10-6 and 10-7** .

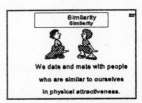

Discuss which factor has the most names. Why do students suppose that is? How much variation is there among the students? What does the individual's set of lists say to them about what most attracts them to others?

4. Use *Activity 2: Interpersonal Attraction* on p.242 of the **ACTIVITY MANUAL** as a good review of the information on attraction theory in this section.

5. Use *Skill-Building Exercise 10.4, Using Affinity-Seeking Strategies* on p. 294-295 of **MESSAGES**. Ask students to identify an instance in their own experience to illustrate each of the strategies. After the students do the application of information, be sure to follow through with the discussion topics as listed. The ethical aspect of some of the affinity-seeking strategies needs to be thoroughly discussed.

6. Ask students to consider what rules they follow in their relationships with each other. How do the rules differ for casual friendships vs. long-term friendships, or for platonic vs. romantic relationships? *Table 10.4: Keeping and Breaking up a Friendship* on pp. 296 of **MESSAGES** will provide some ideas to start the conversation.

7. Place students in two groups. As you read out a type of relationship, each group must place itself in a physical representation of an appropriate model showing depth and breadth of communication according to the social penetration theory. Students may refer to *Figure 10.3* on p. 297 of **MESSAGES** for assistance. **Transparency Master 10-8** will also be helpful.

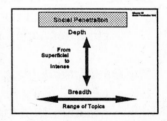

   Some possible relationships to use for this exercise:
   - a. A long time friend from high school
   - b. The checker at the grocery store
   - c. Your minister or rabbi
   - d. Your confessor
   - e. Your mother
   - f. Your spouse
   - g. Your professor
   - h. Your fellow students

8. Ask students to write an analysis of a relationship which deteriorated. Describe the process of depenetration.

---

9.   Use the following model for analyzing the rewards and costs of relationships:
     Relationship   **Rewards**   **Costs**   **Balance**

     Ask students to choose 5 relationships to assess using
     the social exchange theory. **Transparency Master 10-9**
     illustrates Social Exchange Theory.

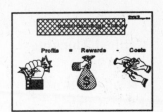

10. Use the model above and carry it a step further.
     Compare the relationships. Are some of the relationships
     alternatives to others?

11. Ask a family or marriage counselor to speak to the class
     about equitable and inequitable relationships. At what
     point in a relationship does inequity become unhealthy?
     At what point does equity become an impossible goal?
     Transparency Master 10-10 will support this
     discussion.

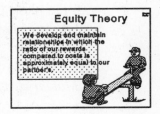

12. Ask someone from Alcoholics Anonymous or Narcotics Anonymous to speak
     about relationships in which one partner pays the costs. How can partners in
     inequitable relationships move toward equity?

Improving Relationship Communication (pp. 300-302)

Emphasis: Learning Objective 4
     Students will be able to explain the suggestions for improving communication in
     relationships.

Emphasis: Skill Objective 3
     Students will improve their abilities to use empathy and self-disclosures, be open
     to change, fight fair, and be reasonable in relationship communication.

Possible Methodologies:
1.   *Activity 1: The Enriched Relationship* on p. 240 of the **ACTIVITY MANUAL**
     will guide students to apply the information in this chapter to improve a
     relationship of their own.

2.   Divide the class into five groups and assign one of the general principles of
     effective communication to each group. Ask the groups to develop three to five

major guidelines to help people apply these principles. Each group should then present its guidelines to the entire class, either in a report or by demonstrating them in action.

Critical Thinking

Possible Methodologies:

1. Compare *Table 10.2: Maintenance Behaviors* on p. 291 of **MESSAGES** to the information about personality types in *Activity 3: What TYPE Are You?* on p. 247 of the **ACTIVITY MANUAL.** How do the examples of each behavior correlate with the likely behaviors of each personality type? Ask students to assess how well these examples describe how they would behave.

2. Assign students to answer the questions in the *Critical Thinking Sidebar: Testing the Matching Hypothesis* on p. 293 of **MESSAGES.**

3. Use the *Critical Thinking Sidebar: Testing the Theory of Rewards and Costs* on p. 298 of **MESSAGES** in the same way. Ask students to answer the questions for themselves, and also for another relationship they have observed.

4. The *Critical Thinking Sidebar: Thinking about Equity in Cultural Perspectives* on p. 299 of **MESSAGES** can stimulate thought about cultural differences related to other theories in this chapter as well. Assign students to choose one section of the chapter and analyze the points in makes in terms of their cross-cultural usefulness.

SKILL EVALUATION

I. Skill Objective 1: Formulate both verbal and nonverbal messages appropriate to your relationship stage

Ask the students to describe a relationship within which they find themselves:
1. What relationship stage are they in?
2. Are they seeking to move the relationship in any direction? If so, in which direction?
3. Plan out a conversation with the other person to accomplish the move and/or to maintain the current stage of the relationship.

II. Skill Objective 2: Assess your own relationships in terms of attraction, rules, social penetration, social exchange, and equity theories.

Use *Skill-Building Exercise 10.5: Applying Theories to Problems* on pp. 299-300 of **MESSAGES** as an evaluation tool.

III.   Skill Objective 3: Use empathy and self-disclosures, be open to change, fight fair, and be reasonable in relationship communication.

Place students in pairs. Each pair will draw two of the skills listed above. Give the pairs the task of writing and presenting two short role-plays in which they demonstrate these skills being used effectively. At the conclusion of the skit, the students should turn in a brief description of the principles applied in the role-plays.

Chapter 11
INTERPERSONAL COMMUNICATION AND CONFLICT

CHAPTER OVERVIEW

Interpersonal conflict refers to a disagreement between or among individuals who have a connection. It can deal with both content and relationship issues. Negative aspects of conflict include thinking of your opponent negatively, depleting your energy, and closing yourself off from the other individual. Positive aspects include examining a problem, working toward a solution, stating what each wants, preventing hostility and resentments from festering.

A model for conflict resolution involves the following stages: define the conflict, define possible solutions, test the solution, evaluate the solution, and accept or reject the solution. In the management of a conflict, individuals may choose avoidance or fighting actively, force or talk, blame or empathy, silencers or facilitating open expression, gunnysacking or present focus, fighting below or above the belt, and verbal aggressiveness and argumentativeness.

Dealing with conflict should be a conscious, careful process. It requires preparing before the conflict and following through after the conflict.

Learning Objectives

After completing this chapter, students should be able to:
1. Define *interpersonal conflict* and distinguish between content and relationship conflict
2. Explain the model of conflict resolution
3. Explain the unproductive and productive conflict strategies
4. Describe the ways to for prepare for and follow up a conflict

---

CLASSROOM APPROACHES

The Nature of Interpersonal Conflict? (pp. 308-312)

Emphasis: Learning Objective 1
Students will be able to define *interpersonal conflict* and distinguish between content and relationship conflict.

Emphasis: Skill Objective 1
Students will improve their abilities to recognize the differences between content and relationship conflicts and respond appropriately to each.

Possible Methodologies:

1. Lecture using information on pp. 308-312 of **MESSAGES**. Use **Transparency Master** 11-1 for support.

2. Introduce the concept of relationship conflict by asking students to privately identify for themselves the two biggest interpersonal conflicts they have or have had. Then ask them to assess the significance of the relationship the conflicts occurred within. They were probably very significant relationships, because differences among people don't lead to conflict unless the differences <u>matter</u>, and they are most likely to matter with people who are significant to you. Discuss the concept of interdependence, and how the more interdependent you are

with someone, the more likely you are to have conflict. All of this discussion should make the point that interpersonal relationships are going to have conflict and that students need not fear it, nor think that the relationship is somehow faulty when it happens.

3. Ask students to write a quick paragraph describing the impact conflict has on relationships. Let volunteers read their paragraphs. Keep track of the number of negative comments about conflict as oppose to the number of positive comments. Most of the comments are likely to be negative; positive ones will be rare. Use these descriptions to lead into a discussion of the myths about conflict (see *Critical Sidebar* on p. 310) and both the negatives and the positives of conflict. **Transparency Masters 11-2** and **11-3** outline some possible negative and positive perspectives.

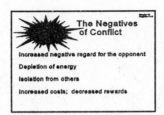
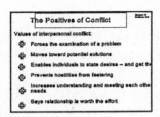

4. Invite   a   guest   from the dispute resolution service in your area. This service is often a not-for-profit effort associated with the municipal or county courts. Ask the speaker to discuss both positive and negative outcomes he/she has observed in the course of resolving disputes.

5. Invite some international students to discuss some of the differences in conflict styles they have experienced between their home country and this one.

6. Use *Skill-Building Exercise 11.1, "Dealing with Conflict Starters,"* on p. 312 of **MESSAGES**. Ask students to share their unproductive responses and then brainstorm productive ones.

A Model of Conflict Resolution (pp. 312-315)

Emphasis: Learning Objective 2

Students will be able to explain the model of conflict resolution.

Emphasis: Skill Objective 2

Students will improve their abilities to deal with interpersonal conflicts in a systematic way.

Possible Methodologies:

1. Lecture using the information on pp. 312-315 of **MESSAGES**. **Transparency Masters 11-4** and **11-5** will be helpful.

2. Develop a conflict scenario. It might be a current political or campus issue, or it might be one a student would like to volunteer for examination. Once you have the scenario, walk it through the steps of the conflict resolution model as follows:

    Divide students into five groups. Each group is responsible for one of the steps in the model. Seat Group 1 at the front of the class and present the scenario to them. With the rest of the class observing, ask them to define the conflict. When they are finished, they will take their seats, and Group 2 will be seated at the front of the room. They are to examine possible solutions. Continue this process until all five steps have been acted out. Then discuss the model and how well it worked. **Transparency Master 11-4** can provide an outline for discussion.

A Conflict Model

3. Use the *Critical Thinking Questions and Cases* question #2 on p. 334 of **MESSAGES**. Choose two competing complaints from the men and the women and apply the conflict resolution model to them. Use the process outlined above in #2, or divide students into small groups to go through the entire model and report back to the class on their solutions.

4. An instrument available for testing ones reaction to conflict is the "Inventory of Anger Communication" by M. J. Bienvenu, Sr. It gives good insight into personal flashpoints. It can be found on p. 81 of the 1976 Annual to **The Handbook of Structured Experiences for Human Relations Training**, University Associates

Publishers and Consultants (8517 Production Avenue, San Diego, California 92121).

5. Demonstrate the *Critical Thinking Sidebar: Three Ways to Look at a Problem* and *Three More Ways to Look at a Problem* on. p. 314 of **MESSAGES** as follows: Divide the class into six groups (or multiples of six if you have a large class). Give each group art supplies (cardboard, construction paper, tape, glue, sequins, feathers, flowers, jewels, ribbons, etc.) and assign each group one of the critical thinking hats. Each group is to create a hat which will illustrate its particular critical thinking technique. When the hats are finished, hold a "style show" for each group to display its hat. As each hat is presented, the group should also provide an example of the critical thinking technique it represents. **Transparency Master 11-5** gives a picture of the six techniques.

6. Use *Activity 3: How to Argue with your Boss* on p. 284 of the **ACTIVITY MANUAL** to allow students to practice using the conflict model. You may also wish to ask them to apply the six critical thinking hats as they consider potential or actual conflicts with a boss.

Conflict Management Strategies (pp. 315-330)

Emphasis: Learning Objective 3
Students will be able to explain the unproductive and productive conflict strategies.

Emphasis: Skill Objective 3
Students will improve their abilities to use more productive conflict strategies and avoid their unproductive counterparts

Possible Methodologies:
1. Lecture using the information on pp. 315-330 in **MESSAGES**. **Transparency Master 11-6** illustrates the information.

2. An entertaining and vivid way to introduce unproductive conflict strategies is to play the game, "Win As Much As You Can" as found on pp. 484-486 of **The**

Interpersonal Communication Book (5th Edition) by Joseph DeVito (New York: Harper & Row, Publishers, Inc.). This exercise is also found on p. 62 of Volume II of **The Handbook of Structured Experiences for Human Relations Training** (La Jolla, CA: University Associates). A similar game is "Circle in the Square" on p. 32 of Volume VI. Both these games dramatize the impact of unproductive strategies and how winning and losing are defined, perceived, and measured.

3. Divide the class into groups of 5-7. Ask each group to decide on a interpersonal conflict situation and then to plan a role-play showing unproductive conflict strategies first, and then showing productive strategies. Let each group present its role-play. After each group, discuss the strategies demonstrated and the impact they have on the relationship. Use **Transparency Master 11-6** to list the strategies.

4. Have students practice identifying conflict strategies by assigning *Skill-Building Exercise 11.2: Increasing Productive Conflict Management* on pp. 326-328 of **MESSAGES**.

5. Assist students with developing skill in giving and receiving criticism by assigning *Activities 2 and 3: Kritikos, Receiving Criticism* and *Kritikos, Giving Criticism* on pp. 276 and 280 of the **ACTIVITY MANUAL**. Assign the reading, *How to Take the Bite Out of Criticism*, on pp. 328-330 of **MESSAGES** to be used with these activities.

6. Suggest that students assess their own relationships. Where there are conflicts, encourage them to try their skills at making the conflict productive. An optional assignment might be to write an analysis of their efforts.

7. Before you begin the section on aggressiveness, have the students take the *Self-Test: How Verbally Aggressive Are You?* on pp. 322-324 of **MESSAGES**.

8. Ask students to collect examples of verbal aggressiveness on television shows they watch and/or in campus conversations. What impact do these statements have on

the relationships within which they occur? **Transparency Master 11-7** illustrates aggressiveness.

4. Before discussing argumentativeness, ask the students to take the *Self-Test: How Argumentative Are You?* on pp. 324-325 of **MESSAGES**. Discuss the results. Does the class get into any arguments in the discussion? If so, discuss that! **Transparency Master 11-8** presents argumentativeness.

5. Assign students to identify people they would assume are aggressive and those they assume are argumentative. What characteristics do the individuals in each group have in common with each other? How do the two groups differ?

Before and After the Conflict (pp. 330-332)

Emphasis: Learning Objective 4
Students will be able to describe the ways to prepare for and follow up on a conflict.

Emphasis: Skill Objective 4
Students will improve their abilities to prepare and follow up interpersonal conflicts as appropriate.

Possible Methodologies:
1. Lecture using information on pp. 330-332 of **MESSAGES**. **Transparency Masters 11-9** and **11-10** provide support.

2. Read *Activity 4: Making a Safe Place for Conflict* on p. 287 of the **ACTIVITY MANUAL** as an introduction to this section on before and after a conflict.

3. Ask students if they have been in a conflict recently. They should apply the ideas for after a conflict and assess both how they feel about the effort and about the impact it had on the relationship.

4. Place students in small groups. Ask for one student in each group to suggest a conflict situation on which the group could work. The situation may be real or

hypothetical. After the situation is described, the group should plan for the conflict by following the suggestions for before the conflict. Then have someone share a conflict which is over. Follow the steps for after the conflict to plan what should happen next. Use **Transparency Masters 11-9** and **11-10** to remind students of the appropriate steps.

Critical Thinking

Possible Methodologies:

1.   Identify a problem -- an issue at your school, in your town, or offered by students. Divide students into groups of six, and ask each person in the group to take responsibility for a different thinking hat (*Critical Thinking Sidebars,* p. 314). The group is to analyze the problem from all six perspectives and offer a solution. All the groups should share their decisions and compare their outcomes. Which thinking hat had the greatest influence in the group discussion? Which hat was hardest to apply? Which one provided the most surprising insight?

2.   Take the same problem as above and use the *Critical Thinking Sidebar: Ghost-Thinking* on p. 315 of **MESSAGES** to analyze it again. Compare the insights gained from the thinking hats with the insights gained from the ghost-thinking team.

3.   Read *Sexual Harassment* on pp. 316-317 of **MESSAGES.** Compare the critical thinking five-stage model (pp.312-315) and/or the conflict management strategies (pp. 315-322) to the suggestions for avoiding sexual harassment and for what to do about sexual harassment. How closely do they compare? Are there suggestions you would add?

4.   Assign the questions in the *Critical Thinking Sidebar: Discovery* on p. 332 of **MESSAGES** to groups of students. Ask them to question students across campus

to discover their opinions. How varied are the responses?

5.   *Activity 5: Messages and Me* on p. 290 of the **ACTIVITY MANUAL** calls students to focus on convergent and divergent thinking.

SKILL EVALUATION

1.   Recognize the differences between content and relationship conflicts and respond appropriately to each

Place students in groups of 3. Provide them with a description of a problem. A current campus controversy or a community issue would be useful. They are to identify potential content issues and potential relationship issues. They should demonstrate, either through role-play or in writing, how they would respond to each of the kinds of issues.

II.   Skill Objective 2: Deal with interpersonal conflicts in a systematic way

Put students in pairs and give them a description of a situation they are to role play. The role play should demonstrate all five steps of the conflict resolution model.

III. Skill Objective 3: Use more productive conflict strategies and avoid their unproductive counterparts

A.   Use *Skill-Building Exercise 11.1* (p. 312) as an evaluation tool.

B.   Give each student three index cards for writing three conflict situations. Collect them from the students and place them in a box. Have each student then come to the front of the room, draw out a card, and provide a possible solution for the conflict and assess whether it would be win-win or win-lose. The extra cards provide an opportunity for a practice round, or substitutes for duplications.

IV.   Skill Objective 4: Prepare and follow up interpersonal conflicts as appropriate

Place students in pairs. They are to play the parts of a couple in a deteriorating relationship. First they should demonstrate ineffective strategies before the conflict, and then they should demonstrate effective ways to prepare before the conflict. Second, they should follow the same demonstration process to illustrate ineffective and effective follow up strategies.

Chapter 12
INTERPERSONAL COMMUNICATION AND POWER

CHAPTER OVERVIEW

Interpersonal power can be studied from three different perspectives: self-esteem, speaking with power, and assertiveness.

Self-esteem, or the way in which we see ourselves, is central to interpersonal power because we are more likely to be effective if we see ourselves as being effective. Self-esteem may be increased by attacking self-destructive beliefs, seeking out nourishing people, working on projects that will lead to success, engaging in self-affirmation, realizing that we do not have to succeed at everything we do, and recognizing that we do not have to be loved by everyone.

Interpersonal power refers to the ability of one person to control the behaviors of another person. Some people are more powerful than others, but all interpersonal messages have a power dimension, and all interpersonal encounters involve power. Often power is exerted through unfair means to manipulate another person. One can learn effective management strategies for dealing with these power plays.

Compliance-gaining strategies are tactics which influence others to do what you want them to do. Compliance-resisting strategies are the tactics which allow you to say "no" and resist attempts to influence you. Compliance gaining and resisting are clear examples of the use of interpersonal power.

Assertiveness, or behavior that enables a person to act in his or her own best interests without stepping on others, is a healthy route to interpersonal power. It is contrasted with nonassertiveness, the tendency to do what others tell you to do without questioning and without concern for what is best for you, and with aggressiveness, or the tendency to take over regardless of the situation.

Learning Objectives

After completing this chapter, students should be able to:
1.   Define *self-esteem* and identify at least five ways of increasing self-esteem

2. Define *power* and explain its major principles and types
3. Explain the popular power plays and how they may be responded to cooperatively
4. Define *assertive, nonassertive,* and *aggressive communication* and explain the principles for increasing assertive communication

Skill Objectives

After completing this chapter, students should improve their abilities to:
1. Increase their own self-esteem
2. Manage power through verbal and nonverbal messages
3. Manage power plays through cooperative responses
4. Increase their own assertiveness (as appropriate)

CLASSROOM APPROACHES

Increasing Self-Esteem (pp. 338-343)

Emphasis: Learning Objective 1
Students will be able to define *self-esteem* and identify at least five ways of increasing self-esteem.

Emphasis: Skill Objective 1
Students will improve their abilities to increase their own self-esteem.

Possible Methodologies:
1. Lecture using the information on pp. 338-343 of **MESSAGES**. **Transparency Masters 12-1** and **12-2** can be used for support. The first two pages are really an introduction to the entire chapter.

2. Lead the class in a consideration of the concept of power. How comfortable are they with it? Any of the following questions to discuss or write about could help students analyze their own reactions: Describe a powerful person. What makes them powerful? Do you like powerful people? Do you aspire to be powerful?

Describe the best powerful person you know. Describe the worst powerful person you know.

3. Ask international students and/or colleagues on campus to discuss the differences in power they encounter between their own culture and that in the United States.

4. Ask students to write a paragraph describing themselves. They should include in it something about their physical, mental, and social lives. What do they like most about themselves? What do they like least? **Transparency Master 12-1** may provide some ideas.

    Put students in small groups of about three each. Ask them to share what they wrote as they feel comfortable about it. On balance, do they assess themselves as having high or low self-esteem?

5. Place posters with the following headings around the room: Parents, Elementary Teachers, High School Teachers, College Teachers, Friends, Brothers/Sisters, Organizations I Belong To, Church/Synagogue. Have students wander from poster to poster and write examples from their own experience with that category which impacted their own self-esteem. The statements may be positive or negative.

    After everyone has had a chance to write on all the posters, conduct a discussion about the how self-esteem is affected by significant others. Read both positive and negative examples from the posters.

6. Discuss the five suggestions in **MESSAGES** for increasing self-esteem. Use *Skill-Building Exercise 12.1: Engaging in Self Affirmation* on p. 342 of **MESSAGES** to practice in affirming oneself. **Transparency Master 12-2** presents the ideas for increasing self-esteem.

7. Put students in groups of about 5-7. Ask them to plan a short skit which demonstrates negative self-esteem and how to begin to make it positive. The skitsshould utilize the six suggestions for increasing self-esteem on pp. 340-342 of **MESSAGES**.

Speaking With Power (pp. 343-359)

Emphasis: Learning Objectives 2 and 3
 Students will be able to:
2. Define *power* and explain its major principles and types
3. Explain the popular power plays and how they may be responded to cooperatively

Emphasis: Skill Objectives 2 and 3
 Students will improve their abilities to:
2. Manage power through verbal and nonverbal messages
3. Manage power plays through cooperative responses

Possible Methodologies:
1. Lecture using the information on pp. 343-359 of **MESSAGES**. Use **Transparency Masters 12-3** through **12-8** for support.

2. Examine the principles of power by asking students to list the most powerful people they can think of both in the past and in the present. Discuss the first principle: some people are more powerful than others. In what ways are the people listed powerful? How did they get their power? Using **Transparency Masters 12-3** and **12-4**, point out the other principles of power. Apply them to the people identified.

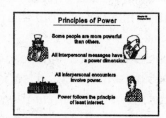

3. Assign students to work in groups of three on an exercise about using powerful speech. Develop a conjugation of statements from powerful to neutral to powerless. For example:

Powerful: This is a great book.

Neutral: I like this book.

Powerless: This, um, is a book I think, er, that you might kind of like, don't you think?

(**Transparency Master 12-5** shows this example.)

As the groups develop their conjugations, they may use *Table 12.1: Toward More Powerful Speech* on pp. 338 of **MESSAGES**. Ask the groups to present their conjugations to the rest of the class with an explanation of what makes the statements powerful, neutral, or powerless.

4. Assign *Activity 1: Interpersonal Persuasion* on p. 299 of the **ACTIVITY MANUAL**. Use the comments from the interviews to introduce the six types of power as listed on pp. 352-353 of **MESSAGES**. Which types were used by the interviewees? How conscious were they of using these types of power?

5. Divide the class into groups of 7. Assign each of them one of the four kinds of power plays found on pp. 349-354 of **MESSAGES**. **Transparency Master 12-6** may be helpful here. They are to plan and present a skit demonstrating the power play and a management strategy for their assigned power play. As each group presents its skit, the rest of the class is to identify the power play. They may also suggest alternative management strategies.

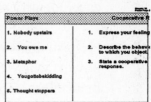

6. Use *Skill-building Exercise 12.3: Managing Power Plays* on p. 354 of **MESSAGES** for further practice of the management strategies for power plays.

7. Put students in pairs. They are each to think of a situation in which they would like to gain compliance. Use **Transparency Master 12-7** to assist in defining compliance-gaining. Together, plan five different compliance-gaining strategies for each other's goal. Ask them to discuss whether the strategy is ethical. Look at

Transparency Master 12-8. What kind of compliance-resisting strategies would be effective against your planned efforts? How might you counter them?

8. Assign students to start a campaign of some sort at their school. Plan the compliance-gaining strategies they wish to use. They are to keep a diary of how the strategies felt and how they worked. They should also identify which compliance-resisting strategies they experience. What happened when compliance-gaining hit compliance-resisting? Which "won"? Why?

9. Invite a politician or political strategist to talk to the class about compliance-gaining strategies used to get votes. What compliance-resisting strategies have they encountered?

10. Use *Activity 2: Getting My Way* on p. 300 of the **ACTIVITY MANUAL**, to gain practice in recognizing compliance-gaining strategies.

11. Ask students to collect examples of compliance-gaining and compliance-resisting for the next class meeting. They may discuss them or role-play them. In either case, identify what they are and how ethical they are.

11. Help students begin to contract with themselves to work toward increasing their power where appropriate. Ask students to make a definite commitment to themselves about an attempt to increase power. Ask them to share it in small groups of three. Plan for the groups to meet again in one week to report to each other on how well they are doing.

12. Assign *Activity 5: Learn to Command Respect* on p. 309 of the **ACTIVITY MANUAL** for students to compare the section in the text on powerful speech with the suggestions on commanding respect.

13. To amplify your discussion of interpersonal power, use John Molloy's book **Molloy's Live for Success**. It has a lengthy discussion with drawings of his research on nonverbal signals which communicate power or lack of it.

Increasing Assertive Communication (pp. 359-363)

Emphasis: Learning Objective 4

Students will be able to define *assertive, nonassertive,* and *aggressive communication* and explain the principles for increasing assertive communication

Emphasis: Skill Objective 4

Students will improve their abilities to increase their own assertiveness (as appropriate).

Possible Methodologies:

1. Lecture using the information on pp. 359-363 of **MESSAGES**. Use **Transparency Masters 12-9** and **12-10** for support.

2. Give students the *Self-Test: How Assertive Are You?* on p. 361 of **MESSAGES**. Lead them to discuss how they feel about their score: do they generally see themselves as consistent with their score? Is this the level of assertiveness they want for themselves? Would they rather be more or less assertive?

3. Put students in groups of three. Ask them to do a conjugation of statements from nonassertive to assertive to aggressive (similar to #3 under the text section, **Speaking with Power,** above). For example:

Nonassertive:	If you want me to do it, I will.
Assertive:	I would be glad to help you out in some other way, but what you have asked is just not something I feel comfortable doing.
Aggressive:	Are you crazy? I wouldn't do that for anything. What do you think I am, anyway?

   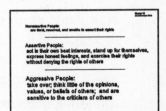

   Transparency Master 12-9 identifies the differences in these three levels.

4. Ask students to write a description of a particular situation in which they would like to be more assertive. Then ask them to write three responses to the situation: nonassertive, assertive and aggressive.

---

5.   Apply the principles for increasing assertiveness (pp. 361-363) to the situations written about in #4 above. **Transparency Master 12-10** lists the principles. Ask students to specifically plan appropriately assertive strategies in their own situations. After students plan their own responses, put them in groups of three. They should then practice their strategies. In the group, two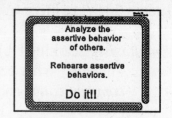
people should role play the situation with the individual who wrote it playing him/herself. The third person should be the observer and give feedback on how well the role players did both verbally and nonverbally. The students should trade roles for each situation so that each person has a chance to play all three parts.

 Critical Thinking

Possible Methodologies:

1.   Assign *Critical Thinking Sidebar: Critically Evaluating Response Strategies* on p. 350 of **MESSAGES.** Ask students to identify situations under which they would use cooperative strategies, those they would ignore, and those they would attempt to neutralize.

2.   The article, *Virtual Communication*, on pp. 357-359 of **MESSAGES** raises some interesting issues related to technological communication. How does this article relate to interpersonal power? Give some specific examples of how technology can be used to increase or decrease power.

3.   Ask students to answer the questions in the *Critical Thinking Sidebar: Being Mindful and Flexible about Assertive Communication* on p. 361 of **MESSAGES.**

4.   The *Critical Thinking Sidebar: Discovery* on p. 363 of **MESSAGES** offers some intriguing questions. Divide the class into four groups and assign one question to each group. The groups should prepare responses with rationales and come to class prepared to lead a class discussion on their question.

SKILL EVALUATION

I.   Skill Objective 1: Increase your own self-esteem

Have students write a brief description of how they would counsel a person with very low self-esteem to use the five strategies for increasing self-esteem.

II.   Skill Objective 2: Manage power through verbal and nonverbal messages

     A.   Assign students to groups of three and have them write a skit demonstrating several appropriate verbal and nonverbal strategies to achieve power. They should turn in a written analysis of their choices.

     B.   Use *Skill-Building Exercise 12.2: Displaying Communication Confidence* as an evaluation tool.

III.   Skill Objective 3:   Manage power plays through cooperative responses

Place students in pairs. They should devise a situation which would call for one of them to gain the compliance of the other by using one of the power plays. They should plan how to ethically use the management strategies on pp. 349-352. Have them take turns acting out the power plays and the management strategies. The "receiving" person may wish to use compliance resistance strategies. When they finish, let them decide on whether the power play or the management strategy "won."

IV.   Skill Objective 4: Increase your own assertiveness (as appropriate)

Ask students to present their plans for improving their assertiveness in a particular situation. They should turn in a written justification for the strategies they use.

Chapter 1   Interpersonal Communication

Multiple-Choice

Choose the one alternative that best completes the statement or answers the question.

Pages: 7
1. In interpersonal communication, people have:
   A) a relationship
   B) a connection
   C) a consciousness of each other
   D) an interaction
   E) all of the above
   Answer: E

Pages: 7
2. Dyads are:
   A) central to interpersonal relationships
   B) disruptive in large groups
   C) subsumed by large groups
   D) small creatures that live in wooded areas
   Answer: A

Pages: 6
3. The five purposes of interpersonal communication are:
   A) learning, playing, helping, connecting and persuading
   B) learning, helping, sensing, analyzing, persuading
   C) relating, playing, influencing, helping, comparing
   D) relating, playing, learning, comparing, helping
   E) influencing, helping, learning, playing, relating
   Answer: E

Pages: 7
4. Interpersonal interactions:
    A) are focused on a single purpose
    B) are frivolous
    C) serve a combination of purposes
    D) are interactions a person holds internally
    E) are all of the above
    Answer: C

Pages: 9
5. "Communication is specific to a given culture" means:
    A) what proves effective in one culture can be specifically used effectively in another
       culture
    B) principles of effective communication are constant across cultures
    C) manners and etiquette are important in communication
    D) principles of effective communication vary from one culture to another.
    Answer: D

Pages: 5
6. The objective of the text, MESSAGES, is:
    A) to provide a formula for behavior
    B) to improve your interpersonal skills
    C) to focus on relevant theory
    D) to allow you to analyze others' behavior
    Answer: B

Pages: 7
7. Which of the following is NOT a major element of interpersonal communication?
    A) source-receiver
    B) context
    C) empathy
    D) noise
    E) feedback
    Answer: C

Pages: 8

8. Your interpersonal competence is:
   A) your knowledge of all the relevant theory
   B) your ability to communicate effectively
   C) your ability to put thoughts and feelings into a code
   D) a special type of message
   Answer: B

Pages: 7-8

9. Which of the following is an encoder?
   A) writer
   B) listener
   C) reader
   D) audience
   Answer: A

Pages: 10

10. Information with which we introduce messages before we send them is:
    A) feedback
    B) encoding
    C) feedforward
    D) psychological noise
    Answer: C

Pages: 10

11. Which of the following is NOT an example of a communication channel:
    A) telephone
    B) smoke signal
    C) face to face contact
    D) ESP
    E) none of the above
    Answer: E

Pages: 10-11
12. Noise is:
    A) semantic
    B) psychological
    C) physical
    D) interference with a message
    E) all of the above
    Answer: E

Pages: 11
13. "Southerners are all rednecks." is an example of which kind of noise?
    A) physical
    B) psychological
    C) semantic
    D) paranoia
    Answer: B

Pages: 12
14. The social-psychological dimension of communication contexts deals with:
    A) status relationships among participants
    B) the sequence of communication events
    C) the rules and norms of the participants
    D) the mental state of the participants
    Answer: A

Pages: 18
15. A transactional process
    A) is an exchange of money
    B) is static
    C) is continuous
    D) has a clear-cut end
    Answer: C

Pages: 19
16. Which statement is NOT true:
    A) there can be no feedback without a receiver
    B) there can be no source without a receiver
    C) there can be no message without a source
    D) there can be no feedforward without feedback
    Answer: D

Pages: 22
17. "We cannot not communicate" is a statement which means:
    A) every aspect of behavior communicates
    B) it takes real effort to avoid communication
    C) in every interaction, someone is strong enough to make sure the other communicates
    D) you can drop out of a communication situation
    E) all of the above
    Answer: A

Pages: 22
18. Saying that communication is irreversible means:
    A) we need to monitor our commitment messages
    B) we have to be careful about messages we may wish to withdraw
    C) we cannot withdraw a message
    D) we sometimes need to defend or justify our behavior
    Answer: C

Pages: 17-23
19. Which of the following is NOT a principle of interpersonal communication:
    A) communication is transactional
    B) communication involves both content and relationship
    C) communication is inevitable
    D) communication is cultureless
    E) communication is unrepeatable
    Answer: D

Pages: 11
20. Which of the following is NOT an example of <u>semantic noise</u>?
    A) different languages
    B) hearing impairments
    C) jargon
    D) giving words different meanings than the speaker intended
    Answer: B

Pages: 12
21. The <u>time dimension</u> of communication context is illustrated in each of the following examples EXCEPT:
    A) telling a joke about time
    B) joking about bombs as you go through the metal detector at an airport
    C) telling a joke about death right after a friend tells you he/she has terminal cancer
    D) telling a friend about the wonders of plastic surgery right after he/she asks your opinion on his/her appearance
    Answer: A

Pages: 12-13
22. Ethical communication requires all of the following EXCEPT:
    A) it supports freedom of choice
    B) it provides accurate information
    C) it is effective
    D) it rests on the notion of options
    Answer: C

Pages: 22
23. The principle of irreversibility has all the following implications EXCEPT:
    A) you need to monitor commitment messages
    B) communication is repeatable
    C) you cannot withdraw a message
    D) what you have communicated remains communicated
    Answer: B

Pages: 18-19
24. "Communication is transactional" means:
    A) there is a financial aspect to all communication
    B) the sender and receiver takes turns playing their roles
    C) each part of communication connects with and depends on the other parts
    D) communication is a linear, clear-cut process
    Answer: C

Pages: 21
25. Arguments are easy to resolve when they involve which dimension of communication:
    A) content
    B) relationship
    C) verbal
    D) nonverbal
    Answer: A

True-False

Write T if the statement is true and F if the statement is false.

Pages: 7
1. Interpersonal communication is communication that only takes place between two people with a close relationship.
   Answer: False

Pages: 7
2. It is impossible to have a two-person communication that is not interpersonal.
   Answer: True

Pages: 22
3. The purposes of interpersonal communication are always conscious and intentional.
   Answer: False

Pages: 22
4. Communication is irreversible.
   Answer: True

Pages: 8
5. For interpersonal communication to occur, meanings must be encoded and decoded.
    Answer: True

Pages: 10
6. Feedforward is when we plan our remarks before we make them.
    Answer: False

Pages: 10-11
7. "Noise" is always physical disruption of a message.
    Answer: False

Pages: 11-12
8. Communication always takes place within a context.
    Answer: True

Pages: 18-19
9. When we analyze interpersonal communication, we need to clearly identify the beginning and end of the transaction.
    Answer: False

Pages: 22
10. You cannot not communicate.
    Answer: True

Short Answer

Write the word or phrase that best completes each statement or answers the question.

Pages: 7
1. Interpersonal communication is communication that takes place between _____ who have a _____.
    Answer: two people; relationship

Pages: 6
2. Interpersonal communication serves five important purposes:
    Answer: to learn, relate, influence, play, help

Pages: 6

3. The purpose of "Play" is to _____ from work and to _____ yourself.
   Answer: escape; enjoy

Pages: 19

4. We communicate both content and _____ messages.
   Answer: relationship

Pages: 8

5. The act of producing messages is termed _____ and the act of understanding messages is termed _____.
   Answer: encoding, decoding

Pages: 10-11

6. Biases and prejudices are examples of _____.
   Answer: psychological noise

Pages: 11-12

7. The four dimensions of context are:
   Answer: physical, cultural, social-psychological, temporal

Pages: 12

8. The principles of effective communication _____ from one culture to another; what will prove effective in one culture may prove _____ in another.
   Answer: vary, ineffective

Pages: 12

9. There is a _____ aspect to any interpersonal communication.
   Answer: right vs. wrong

Pages: 19

10. The interpersonal communication process is _____.
    Answer: continuous

Essay

Write your answer in the space provided or on a separate sheet of paper.

Pages: 6
1. Give an example of each of the five purposes for interpersonal communication.
   Answer: Learning about the world, others, and yourself
   Building relationships
   Influencing others
   Playing
   Helping

Pages: 7-16
2. What are the essential elements of interpersonal communication? How does the concept of transactional communication tie these elements together?
   Answer: Source-receiver, messages, feedback, feedforward, channel, noise, context, competence, ethics

   Each part of the communication act connects with and depends on each other part.

Pages: 11-12
3. Discuss the impact of context on communication. Give examples of impact from two different dimensions of context.
   Answer: Communication always takes place within a context and is influenced by it. The dimensions of context are cultural, social- psychological, and temporal.

Chapter 2   The Self

Multiple-Choice

Choose the one alternative that best completes the statement or answers the question.

Pages: 31-32
1. The Johari window has four quadrants containing four different selves:
   A) hidden, blind, social, open
   B) open, hidden, unknown, social
   C) unknown, blind, hidden, open
   D) unknown, social, blind, aware
   Answer: C

Pages: 31
2. Which self represents all the things about yourself that other know but of which you are ignorant?
   A) unknown
   B) blind
   C) open
   D) hidden
   E) social
   Answer: B

Pages: 31
3. Which self represents all that things that characterize you and that both you and others know about you?
   A) hidden
   B) social
   C) blind
   D) open
   E) aware
   Answer: D

Pages: 31
4. Which self represents all that you know of yourself but that you keep to yourself?
   A) open
   B) unknown
   C) blind
   D) aware
   E) hidden
   Answer: E

Pages: 32
5. Which self represents truths that exist but that neither you nor others know?
   A) unknown
   B) hidden
   C) blind
   D) social
   E) open
   Answer: A

Pages: 34
6. Asking yourself about yourself is:
   A) egocentric
   B) a way to increase your open self
   C) a way to increase self awareness
   D) counter-productive
   Answer: C

Pages: 39
7. Self-disclosure is a way of
   A) revealing the hidden self
   B) boring other people
   C) increasing self-awareness
   D) increasing self-acceptance
   Answer: A

8. Self-disclosure involves all EXCEPT:
    A) new knowledge
    B) at least one other individual
    C) reciprocation
    D) conspicuousness
    Answer: D

9. We are more likely to self-disclose under all the following circumstances EXCEPT:
    A) when we are with people we like
    B) when the other person self-discloses
    C) when we are in small groups
    D) when we are feeling less competent
    Answer: D

10. Apparently, meaningful relationships cannot develop without:
    A) apprehension
    B) being self aware
    C) revealing your hidden self
    D) self-disclosure
    Answer: D

11. Recent research shows that people who are able to confide in others about troubled feelings or a traumatic event:
    A) increase their hidden self
    B) are less vulnerable to illnesses
    C) may be seen as mischievous or antagonistic
    D) don't have to be thinking of the other person's feelings
    Answer: B

Pages: 42
12. You should self-disclose out of a concern for:
    A) the relationship
    B) yourself
    C) others involved
    D) all of the above
    Answer: D

Pages: 42-46
13. You should self-disclose only if:
    A) it is appropriate
    B) there is a desire to improve the relationship
    C) it imposes no burdens
    D) the other person is also disclosing
    E) all of the above
    Answer: E

Pages: 46
14. Lack of reciprocity on self-disclosure is:
    A) deferring to the one who wishes to disclose
    B) a natural balance
    C) important feedback from the other person
    D) a desire to hurt or punish
    E) all of the above
    Answer: C

Pages: 47
15. When someone discloses to you,
    A) it is a sign of trust
    B) it imposes a burden
    C) it requires you to disclose in return
    D) he or she is trying to hurt you
    Answer: A

Pages: 47
16. There are three guidelines for responding to self-disclosure:
    A) respond back immediately, support the discloser, listen actively
    B) listen actively, don't use the disclosure against the other person, support the
       discloser
    C) support the discloser, keep it confidential, listen actively
    D) don't get involved in disclosing yourself, support the discloser, keep it confidential
    Answer: C

Pages: 28-29
17. Your self-concept develops from at least these three primary sources:
    A) books you read, your parents, your own interpretations
    B) social comparisons, other's images of you, your own interpretations
    C) other's images of you, movies/films/pictures, social comparisons
    D) your own interpretations, social comparisons, physical activities
    Answer: B

Pages: 40-41
18. Appropriate reasons for self-disclosure include all of the following EXCEPT:
    A) insight into who you are
    B) a chance to brag
    C) enhances relationships
    D) increases ability to deal with problems
    Answer: B

Pages: 49
19. According to surveys of college students, what percentage indicate they suffer "severe,
    debilitating communication apprehension?"
    A) 5%
    B) 25%
    C) 10-20%
    D) 20-30%
    Answer: C

Pages: 49
20. Communication apprehension is NOT:
    A) a common handicap
    B) a disadvantage on the job
    C) sometimes debilitating
    D) a symptom of ineffective, unhappy people
    Answer: D

Pages: 50
21. With regard to dating:
    A) apprehensives avoid it entirely
    B) apprehensives date many different people to avoid relationships
    C) apprehensives engage more in steady dating
    D) apprehensives seek out new people to date
    Answer: C

Pages: 50
22. Which of the following is NOT a characteristic of high apprehensives?
    A) less likely to hold position of leadership
    B) are more satisfied in their jobs
    C) earn poorer grades
    D) less desirous of advancement in their jobs
    Answer: B

Pages: 51
23. The more unpredictable the situation,
    A) the less time to get apprehensive
    B) the more conspicuous one is
    C) the greater ones apprehension
    D) the more we are evaluated
    Answer: C

Pages: 51
24. Focusing on success involves all EXCEPT:
    A) thinking positively
    B) concentrate on doing your best job
    C) seeing yourself failing
    D) seeing yourself succeeding
    Answer: C

158

Pages: 51
25. Putting communication apprehension in perspective means:
    A) other people can't perceive your apprehension as sharply as you do
    B) the world will end if you don't succeed
    C) people are just waiting for you to fail
    D) you are the only one who feels the way you do
    Answer: A

True-False

Write T if the statement is true and F if the statement is false.

Pages: 31
1. The blind self of the Johari window contains all that you know of yourself but that you keep to yourself.
    Answer: False

Pages: 32
2. The unknown self quadrant represents all the things about yourself that others know but of which you are ignorant.
    Answer: False

Pages: 34
3. To each person who knows you, you are a somewhat different person.
    Answer: True

Pages: 39
4. To tell someone something about yourself that he or she already knows would not be self-disclosure.
    Answer: True

Pages: 40
5. Generally, women disclose themselves less than men do.
    Answer: False

Pages: 40
6. Self-disclosure enhances the meaningfulness of relationships.
    Answer: True

Pages: 46
7. Appropriate self-disclosures include honest expressions which will hurt or punish the other person.
Answer: False

Pages: 49
8. Communication apprehension is probably the most common handicap suffered by people in contemporary American society.
Answer: True

Pages: 51
9. The more we can predict what is going to happen in a situation, the more likely we are to feel apprehensive.
Answer: False

Pages: 51
10. Reducing negative assumptions helps reduce apprehension.
Answer: True

Short Answer

Write the word or phrase that best completes each statement or answers the question.

Pages: 30
1. The Johari window is particularly helpful in enabling us to increase our

_____.
Answer: self-awareness

Pages: 30
2. Self-awareness gives us _____ over ourselves.
Answer: control

Pages: 31
3. Actively seek out information to reduce your _____ self.
Answer: blind

Pages: 39

4. Self-disclosure is a type of communication in which you _____ information about _____ that you normally keep hidden.
   Answer: reveal; yourself

Pages: 39

5. What one person in a dyad does, the other person does as a response. This is the _____.
   Answer: dyadic effect

Pages: 41

6. Couples who engage in significant self-disclosure are found to _____ than couples who do not.
   Answer: remain together longer

Pages: 41

7. Self-disclosure promotes _____ health.
   Answer: physiological

Pages: 42

8. Each person has to make his or her own decisions concerning _____.
   Answer: self-disclosures

Pages: 46

9. During your self-disclosures, give the other person a chance to _____.
   Answer: reciprocate

Essay

Write your answer in the space provided or on a separate sheet of paper.

Pages: 31-32

1. Explain how the four quadrants of the Johari window relate to each other.
   Answer: As one quadrant changes, the other three must change as well.

Pages: 33

2. How can you increase your self-awareness?
   Answer: Listen to others
             Seek information about yourself
             Increase your open self

Pages: 40-42

3. Contrast the rewards and dangers of self-disclosure.
   Answer: Rewards: increases knowledge of self increases communication effectiveness
             enhances meaningful relationships

             Dangers:decreases mutual attraction provides information which can be used
             against you leads to negative evaluations

Pages: 50-51

4. Give some specific suggestions for managing communication apprehension.
   Answer: Acquire skills and experience
             Focus on success
             Reduce unpredictability
             Put apprehension in perspective

Chapter 3   Perception in Interpersonal Communication

Multiple-Choice

Choose the one alternative that best completes the statement or answers the question.

Pages: 60
1. Interpersonal perception is:
   A) a one-to-one relationship
   B) a way of seeing from the other person's point of view
   C) a way of sensing, organizing, and interpreting data about people
   D) an external rather than internal process
   Answer: C

Pages: 60 - 63
2. The stages of perception are:
   A) sense, organize, interpret-evaluate
   B) interpret-evaluate, sense, organize
   C) organize, sense, interpret-evaluate
   D) proximity, similarity, interpretation
   Answer: A

Pages: 61
3. Our senses are bombarded with stimuli. Consequently, we
   A) look for similarities
   B) select and attend to those which meet our immediate needs
   C) systematically process all of it
   D) organize it just like everyone else does
   Answer: B

Pages: 63 - 76
4. We make judgments about others on the basis of all the following EXCEPT:
   A) stereotypes
   B) first impressions
   C) seeing them from their point of view
   D) implicit theories
   Answer: C

Pages: 65
5. Relying on early information for a general idea of what a person is like is also called:
A) stereotypes
B) our first impressions
C) prophecies we make
D) implicit theories
Answer: B

Pages: 72
6. Seeing a person primarily as having the characteristics of a group is also called:
A) our first impressions
B) prophecies we make
C) implicit theories
D) stereotypes
Answer: D

Pages: 68 - 69
7. A subconscious set of rules that tells us which personal traits go with others is also called:
A) prophecies we make
B) implicit theories
C) our first impressions
D) stereotypes
Answer: B

Pages: 69 - 71
8. Giving subtle cues or hints about how we expect the other person to act is also called:
A) stereotypes
B) implicit theories
C) prophecies we make
D) our first impressions
Answer: C

Pages: 65
9. If what comes last in a sequence exerts the most influence in a communication situation, we have a:
    A) primacy effect
    B) self-fulfilling prophecy
    C) recency effect
    D) stereotype
    Answer: C

Pages: 70
10. Acting as if a prediction were true is called a:
    A) recency effect
    B) primacy effect
    C) stereotype
    D) self-fulfilling prophecy
    Answer: D

Pages: 72
11. A stereotype is all of the following EXCEPT:
    A) a printing term
    B) a fixed impression of a group of people
    C) a way to identify individuality
    D) a distortion of our ability to perceive people accurately
    Answer: C

Pages: 65
12. First impressions are all of the following EXCEPT:
    A) unjust
    B) inevitable
    C) highly accurate
    D) a filter
    Answer: C

Pages: 71
13. The very same behavior will be evaluated positively or negatively:
    A) depending on the circumstances others infer to be related to the behavior
    B) at the same time
    C) only extremely rarely
    D) if the person being evaluated is perceived as neurotic
    Answer: A

Pages: 68 - 69
14. Assumptions about personality traits that go with other traits are called:
    A) misperceptions
    B) prophecies
    C) implicit theories
    D) perspective taking
    Answer: C

Pages: 69 - 70
15. Prophecies are all of the following EXCEPT:
    A) inevitable
    B) infrequent
    C) influences on behavior
    D) reciprocal
    Answer: B

Pages: 72
16. Stereotypes cause us to do all of the following EXCEPT:
    A) put people in boxes
    B) prevent seeing a person's individuality
    C) see a person as one of "them"
    D) focus on unique characteristics
    Answer: D

Pages: 77
17. You can increase your accuracy in interpersonal perception by:
    A) using stereotypes
    B) relying on first impressions
    C) observing and interacting with people
    D) trusting the implicit theories in your head
    Answer: C

18. Perception checking consists of which two steps:
    A) describing tentatively and asking for confirmation
    B) evaluating descriptively and asking for confirmation
    C) describing tentatively and proving your initial perception is correct
    D) interpreting another's feelings and elaborating on those feelings
    Answer: A

19. Which of the following steps would be appropriate in interaction with a blind person?
    A) ignore a blind person on the street to avoid being condescending
    B) always ask before you try to help
    C) avoid expressions such as "see you later" or "did you see that?"
    D) leave doors half open so that the blind person doesn't have to search for the knob
    Answer: B

20. When a variety of cues about a person all point in the same direction,
    A) you can feel comfortable about "mindreading"
    B) you can be sure that you are not biased
    C) you can form positive conclusions
    D) you stand a better chance of making accurate judgments
    Answer: D

21. A major goal of critical thinking is:
    A) to teach us to be judgmental
    B) to avoid dogmatic people
    C) to perceive and make sense of what exists
    D) to better understand art, music and drama
    Answer: C

22. Generally research shows that if we feel people are in control of negative behaviors,
    A) we feel sorry for them
    B) we do not blame them for their negative circumstances
    C) we identify with them
    D) we will come to dislike them
    Answer: D

Pages: 75
23. A self-serving bias
    A) helps you understand others better
    B) causes you to evaluate yourself more positively than others would
    C) is a self-fulfilling prophecy
    D) is a highly accurate insight
    Answer: B

Pages: 60
24. "People perception" is the process by which
    A) we as people perceive
    B) stimuli impinge on our senses
    C) people impact us
    D) we become aware of and interpret-evaluate the traits of people
    Answer: D

Pages: 78
25. Perhaps the most important rule to follow to increase your accuracy in people perception is:
    A) check your perceptions
    B) act on your assumptions
    C) rely on implicit personality theory
    D) be aware of primacy-recency effects
    Answer: A

True-False

Write T if the statement is true and F if the statement is false.

Pages: 60
1. Perhaps the most important principle of interpersonal communication is that we each see the world and interpret it from our own point of view.
   Answer: True

Pages: 60
2. Perception takes place in one quick step.
   Answer: False

Pages: 62

3. We tend to perceive things that are physically similar as belonging together.
   Answer: True

Pages: 65

4. The most important thing that we perceive is referred to as the "primacy effect."
   Answer: False

Pages: 70

5. A "self-fulfilling prophecy" is one which occurs when you make a prediction that comes true because you made the prediction and acted as if it were already true.
   Answer: True

Pages: 72

6. Stereotypes point up unique characteristics of individuals within a group.
   Answer: False

Pages: 65

7. It is important to form conclusions about people quickly in order to guide your interactions.
   Answer: False

Pages: 78

8. Asking the other person if your perceptions of their behavior are accurate is a faux pas.
   Answer: False

Pages: 60-63

9. In person perception, we interpret the immediate environment, collect sense data, and then organize it.
   Answer: False

Pages: 76-77

10. The goal of perception checking is to prove that your initial perception is correct.
    Answer: False

Short Answer

Write the word or phrase that best completes each statement or answers the question.

Pages: 60

1. _____ is the process by which we become aware of some of the many stimuli bombarding our senses.
    Answer: perception

Pages: 60

2. _____ concerns the way we sense, organize, and interpret-evaluate information about people.
    Answer: interpersonal or people perception

Pages: 62

3. The principle of _____ says that we perceive things that are physically similar as belonging together.
    Answer: similarity

Pages: 62

4. The principle of _____ says that we perceive things that are physically close together as a unit.
    Answer: proximity

Pages: 63

5. The third stage of perception, interpretation-evaluation, is a highly _____ process.
    Answer: subjective

Pages: 65

6. If information or stimuli that comes to you first exerts the most influence on your perception, you are experiencing a _____ effect.
    Answer: primacy

Pages: 65

7. If information or stimuli that comes to you last exerts the most influence on your perception, you are experiencing a _____ effect.
    Answer: recency

Pages: 69 - 70
8. A prediction that comes true because you made the prediction and acted as if it were true is called a _____.
   Answer: self-fulfilling prophecy

Pages: 72
9. A fixed impression of a group of people is called a _____.
   Answer: stereotype

Pages: 68-69
10. Theories about personality traits that go with other traits are called _____.
    Answer: implicit theories

Essay

Write your answer in the space provided or on a separate sheet of paper.

Pages: 63 - 76
1. Explain the five psychological processes that influence perceptions and the barriers to accurate perception in which each of them results.
   Answer: primacy and recency (first impressions), the self- fulfilling prophecy (prophecies), implicit personality theory (implicit theories), stereotyping, and attribution

Pages: 60 - 63
2. Explain the stages we go through in perception.
   Answer: sensing, organizing, interpreting-evaluating

Pages: 76-79
3. How can we check the accuracy of our perceptions?
   Answer: describe in tentative terms what you think is happening; ask the other person for confirmation

172

Chapter 4   Listening in Interpersonal Communication

Multiple-Choice

Choose the one alternative that best completes the statement or answers the question.

Pages: 99-100
1. Which of the following is NOT a technique of active listening?
    A) Ask relevant questions
    B) Assimilate
    C) Paraphrase
    D) Express understanding of emotions
    Answer: B

Pages: 81
2. Which communication activity occupies the most time?
    A) Speaking
    B) Reading
    C) Listening
    D) Writing
    Answer: C

Pages: 94
3. "Leveling" means:
    A) Reconstructing messages so that they reflect your own attitudes and values
    B) Distorting messages because of our position or negative attitudes toward the other
       person
    C) One or two aspects of the message is high-lighted, emphasized, and perhaps embellished
    D) Complex messages are simplified so that they are easier to remember
    Answer: D

Pages: 92-93
4. In empathic listening, we do all of the following EXCEPT:
   A) listen from the speaker's point of view
   B) respond to the speaker's needs rather than our own
   C) engage in dialogue, not monologue
   D) view the speaker as an equal
   E) lose our own identity and assume the identity of the other person
   Answer: E

Pages: 93
5. "Offensive listening" means:
   A) finding fault with the speaker's messages
   B) removing physical barriers to communication
   C) actively directing the conversation
   D) listening only when your team has possession of the ball
   Answer: A

Pages: 92-93
6. A particularly empathic response is
   A) "Don't feel so bad."
   B) "In time you'll forget all about this."
   C) "Cheer up."
   D) "You must feel really hurt."
   Answer: D

Pages: 91
7. Passive listening is:
   A) without merit
   B) a refusal to self-disclose
   C) listening without talking or directing the speaker nonverbally
   D) when you are emotionally and intellectually ready to engage in the sharing of meaning
   Answer: C

Pages: 82
8. Receiving:
   A) is the same as hearing
   B) causes you to focus on the speaker rather than on what you plan to say
   C) ends with accepting the message the speaker sends
   D) deals only with verbal messages
   Answer: B

Pages: 95
9. Mixed messages:
   A) deal with content and relationship
   B) indicate poor logic
   C) communicate two contradictory things
   D) reveal emotion
   Answer: C

Pages: 97-98
10. Which of the following is NOT a function of active listening:
    A) allows the listener to be sure he/she understands what the speaker meant
    B) stimulates speaker to explore feelings and thoughts
    C) allows the listener to control the conversation
    D) accepts the speaker's feelings
    Answer: C

Pages: 94
11. Critical listening is:
    A) biased
    B) analyzing and evaluating messages
    C) judging the other speaker
    D) negative
    Answer: B

Pages: 98-99
12. Which sentence below is an acceptable paraphrase of the statement, "I failed the test. I might as well drop out of school."
    A) Don't feel so bad; you'll do better next time.
    B) If you had studied instead of going out the night before, you'd have done O.K.
    C) I've failed tests, too. I know how bad it feels.
    D) Because you failed the test, you feel like a failure in college.
    Answer: D

Pages: 94
13. Sharpening is:
    A) active listening
    B) non-verbal
    C) emphasizing details
    D) reducing the message to a more simplified form
    Answer: C

Pages: 92-93
14. Communicating empathically means
    A) supporting your own ideas
    B) supporting the speaker
    C) agreeing with whatever the speaker says
    D) providing needed resources
    Answer: B

Pages: 94
15. Which of the following is NOT required in listening with an open mind?
    A) focus on verbal and nonverbal feedback
    B) sharpening
    C) listening to what speakers omit
    D) listening for the speaker's biases
    Answer: B

Pages: 90
16. Buzzwords are:
    A) labels like "feminist"
    B) effective shortcuts
    C) ways to avoid emotion
    D) ways to clarify thinking
    Answer: A

Pages: 89
17. Controlling distractions means all of the following EXCEPT:
    A) planning for uninterrupted time
    B) postponing calls
    C) using effective nonverbal communication
    D) doing most of the speaking
    Answer: D

Pages: 93
18. Objective listening is:
    A) preoccupation with self
    B) offensive listening
    C) listening with detachment
    D) telling a friend how the world hates him or her
    Answer: C

Pages: 94
19. Assimilation is:
    A) hearing what's expected
    B) assuming value in what the speaker says
    C) reconstructing the message to reflect your beliefs and values
    D) noise
    Answer: C

Pages: 94
20. Leveling is:
    A) one or two aspects of a message are highlighted
    B) the message is simplified
    C) assuming value
    D) dramatic detail
    Answer: B

Pages: 82
21. A preoccupation with self or what you will say next is an example of
    A) assimilation
    B) active listening
    C) listening obstacles
    D) feedforward
    Answer: C

Pages: 81
22. Listening can be defined as:
    A) A process of putting together into some meaningful whole the listener's understanding of the speaker's total message
    B) An active process of receiving, understanding, remembering, evaluating, and responding to aural stimuli
    C) An automatic response within earshot of auditory stimuli
    D) A passive reception of auditory stimuli
    Answer: B

Pages: 92-93
23. Empathic listening can be defined as:
    A) Listening without judgment or evaluation; listening for understanding
    B) The procedure whereby details of what we have heard become heightened and emphasized
    C) Placing ourselves into the position of the speaker so that we feel as the speaker feels
    D) Information that is sent by a listener telling the speaker how the listener is reacting to what the speaker is saying
    Answer: C

Pages: 93
24. All but one of the following are ways ofachieving empathy:
    A) role-play the other person
    B) put yourself in the shoes of the other person
    C) engage in dialogue
    D) interrupt the other
    Answer: D

True-False

Write T if the statement is true and F if the statement is false.

Pages: 92
1. When we listen empathically, we listen from our own point of view.
    Answer: False

Pages: 93
2. Empathic listening requires understanding emotionally.
    Answer: True

Pages: 98-99
3. Reflecting back the speaker's feelings is insulting.
    Answer: False

Pages: 89
4. Controlling distractions is helpful in setting a supportive listening climate.
    Answer: True

Pages: 95
5. A mixed message communicates contradictory meanings.
    Answer: True

Pages: 98-100
6. Three techniques in the process of active listening are questioning, paraphrasing and expressing understanding.
    Answer: True

Pages: 98-99
7. Stating in your own words what you think the speaker meant will only confuse the message.
    Answer: False

Pages: 95
8. Communication has both a surface meaning and a deeper one.
    Answer: True

Pages: 95
9. Focus on relationship and content messages.
   Answer: True

Pages: 98-99
10. Reflection back to the speaker is unnecessary.
    Answer: False

Short Answer

Write the word or phrase that best completes each statement or answers the question.

Pages: 82
1. The five main purposes for listening are:
   Answer: to help, to learn, to relate, to play, to influence

Pages: 97
2. Active listening is a process of putting into some meaningful _____ the listener's understanding of the speaker's _____ and _____.
   Answer: whole, thoughts, feelings

Pages: 93
3. List three suggestions for listening with empathy:
   Answer: Seek to understand both thoughts and feelings
             Avoid offensive listening
             Beware of friend or foe factors

Pages: 95
4. Mixed messages communicate _____ feelings.
   Answer: contradictory

Pages: 81
5. The communication activity on which we spend the most time is _____.
   Answer: listening

Pages: 95-96

6. List three suggestions for dealing with mixed messages:
   Answer: Listen to verbal and non-verbal messages.
   Listen to content and relationship messages.
   Confront mixed messages in a non-threatening way.
   (or: Listen to what speakers omit.)

Pages: 82

7. The five reasons for listening are _____, _____, _____, _____ and _____.
   Answer: to learn, to relate, to influence, to play, to help

Pages: 87

8. Responses made back to a speaker should:
   Answer: be supportive of the speaker by using back-channeling cues
   express support in final responses
   own your own responses - use "I" messages

Pages: 81-87

9. The five steps in the listening process are:
   Answer: receiving, understanding, remembering, evaluating, responding

Pages: 91-95

10. You can increase your listening effectiveness by:
    Answer: participatory and passive listening
    empathic and objective listening
    nonjudgmental and critical listening
    surface and depth listening

Essay

Write your answer in the space provided or on a separate sheet of paper.

Pages: 81-82

1. Contrast listening and hearing.
   Answer: Hearing automatically occurs within earshot of auditory stimuli; listening requires energy, effort, skills, active involvement of both sender and receiver.

Pages: 91-92

2. Explain what makes listening participatory:

   Answer: work at listening, use thought-speech time difference effectively, use nonverbal behaviors which indicate physical alertness, beware of hearing what's expected, beware of preoccupation with yourself

Pages: 85-86

3. What is evaluating? How do you evaluate effectively?

   Answer: A step in listening which involves judging the message.
   Suggestions: Resist until you fully understand, assume the speaker has goodwill, distinguish fact from inference, indentify any bias or self-interest from the speaker

Pages: 98-101

4. Explain the techniques of active listening.

   Answer: paraphrase the speaker's thoughts
   express understanding
   ask questions

Chapter 5   Verbal Messages

Multiple-Choice

Choose the one alternative that best completes the statement or answers the question.

Pages: 110-118
1. Which of the following is NOT a characteristic of meaning?
    A) it is in our minds
    B) it is contextual
    C) it is objective
    D) it is in clusters
    Answer: C

Pages: 113-114
2. Which of the following is NOT an example of a high order abstraction?
    A) visual art
    B) "Forest Gump"
    C) film
    D) cinematography
    Answer: B

Pages: 113-114
3. Choose the term which is the least abstract:
    A) personnel analyst
    B) job
    C) occupation
    D) career
    Answer: A

Pages: 113-114
4. Choose the term which is the most abstract:
    A) hobby
    B) wood carving
    C) leisure activity
    D) painting
    Answer: C

Pages: 119-120

5. Examples of polarization include all EXCEPT:
   A) for or against
   B) educated and uneducated
   C) either, or
   D) attending school, working
   Answer: D

Pages: 121

6. An example of extensional orientation is:
   A) getting sick when told that one's dinner was frog legs, not chicken
   B) fighting someone who calls you a name
   C) eating only when you are hungry
   D) checking your watch to see if it is time to eat
   Answer: C

Pages: 121

7. An example of an inference is:
   A) she is wearing a red hat
   B) he is lazy
   C) he is fat
   D) she is a blonde
   Answer: B

Pages: 121-123

8. Factual statements:
   A) approach certainty
   B) may be about any time
   C) may be made by anyone
   D) involve varying degrees of probability
   Answer: A

Pages: 128

9. Disconfirmation is a communication pattern in which you:
   A) disagree with a person
   B) are unwilling to accept what someone says
   C) acknowledge someone's significance
   D) ignore someone's presence
   Answer: D

Pages: 128-129
10. Confirmation is a communication pattern in which you:
    A) say what someone has to say is not worth serious attention
    B) disagree with the person
    C) accept a person's definition of self
    D) ignore someone's presence
    Answer: C

Pages: 129
11. A technique which is disconfirming is:
    A) reflect back the speaker's thoughts and feelings
    B) ask questions
    C) take issue with what the other says
    D) quickly interpret or evaluate what the other says
    Answer: D

Pages: 123
12. When we make judgments of the whole based on only a part, we are
    A) creating polarization
    B) using allness
    C) bypassing
    D) assuming things stay the same
    Answer: B

Pages: 123
13. When we focus on similarities and ignore differences, we are
    A) demonstrating an intentional orientation
    B) bypassing
    C) being indiscriminate
    D) demonstrating allness
    Answer: C

Pages: 121-123
14. When we make statements about what we have not observed, we are
    A) bypassing
    B) giving primary importance to labels
    C) being indiscriminate
    D) making inferences
    Answer: D

Pages: 132-134
15. Which of the following is NOT an example of linguistic sexism?
    A) mailman
    B) man-made
    C) human
    D) chairman
    Answer: C

Pages: 129
16. Confirming language
    A) places a particular group in an inferior position
    B) accepts all people
    C) is sexist
    D) ignores lack of clarity in the other's remarks
    Answer: B

Pages: 132-134
17. Which of the following is an example of sexist language?
    A) actress
    B) chairperson
    C) he/she
    D) Mr.
    Answer: A

Pages: 131-132
18. Which of the following expressions is not racist?
    A) black night
    B) black violinist
    C) the choice is black and white
    D) that's white of you
    Answer: A

Pages: 131
19. Non-racist language:
    A) expresses racist attitudes
    B) contributes to developing racist attitudes
    C) does not place an ethnic group in an inferior position
    D) emphasizes differences
    Answer: C

Pages: 134-135
20. Heterosexism is
    A) language used to reinforce homosexual attitudes
    B) refers to men only
    C) is too new to be clearly identified
    D) is based on the presumption of heterosexuality
    Answer: D

Pages: 123-125
21. Which of the following messages is indiscrimination?
    A) Politicians are all liars.
    B) You never call me.
    C) You're either a hawk or a dove.
    D) She hates me.
    Answer: A

Pages: 125-127
22. Which of the following would you NEVER say to someone (according to George Thompson)?
    A) asking what's the matter
    B) explaining why you must keep a confidence
    C) saying, "this may be difficult to understand"
    D) asking, "Why won't you be reasonable?"
    Answer: D

Pages: 121
23. Extensional orientation is:
    A) when speaker and listener miss each other with their meanings
    B) giving primary attention to the real world rather than to the world of words
    C) treating inferences as if they were facts
    D) giving primary attention to labels
    Answer: B

Pages: 123
24. Static evaluation is:
    A) the failure to acknowledge the other person or that person's definition of self
    B) the failure to distinguish the uniqueness among items because they are all labeled by the same term
    C) the denial of change
    D) the tendency to divide the world into two extreme categories
    Answer: C

True-False

Write T if the statement is true and F if the statement is false.

Pages: 113-114
1. Meaning is abstract.
   Answer: True

Pages: 115
2. Meanings are communicated in packages.
   Answer: True

Pages: 111
3. Snarl and purr words describe whether something is good or bad.
   Answer: False

Pages: 119-120
4. "You are now either taking a test or you are not taking a test." This statement is an example of appropriate polarization.
   Answer: True

Pages: 121
5. Extensional Orientation is the tendency to stretch meanings beyond their original intent.
   Answer: False

Pages: 121-122
6. There is nothing wrong with making inferential statements.
   Answer: True

Pages: 114-115
7. The cultural context will influence whether a meaning is friendly or not.
    Answer: True

Pages: 123
8. The tendency to end your statements with the expression "etc." is an example of allness.
    Answer: False

Pages: 132-133
9. The use of masculine pronouns as generic references is an indication of the extent of linguistic sexism.
    Answer: True

Pages: 134-135
10. Heterosexism is language used to disparage heterosexuals.
    Answer: False

Short Answer

Write the word or phrase that best completes each statement or answers the question.

Pages: 111
1. Look for meanings in _____, not in _____.
    Answer: people, words

Pages: 110
2. Meanings are communicated _____ and _____.
    Answer: verbally and nonverbally

Pages: 114
3. Verbal and nonverbal messages exist in a _____ which largely determines their _____.
    Answer: context, meaning

Pages: 111
4. Snarl words and purr words do not _____ people or events in the real world but the speaker's _____ about those people and events.
    Answer: describe, feelings

Pages: 119-121
5. Correcting polarization: use _____.
   Answer: middle terms

Pages: 121-123
6. One way to avoid embarrassing ourselves with inferences is to use _____
   phrases.
   Answer: tentative

Pages: 129
7. To correct disconfirmation, acknowledge the presence of _____.
   Answer: the other person

Pages: 123
8. To correct static evaluation, focus on _____; _____ your statements.
   Answer: change, date

Pages: 124
9. To correct indiscrimination, _____ your terms.
   Answer: index

Pages: 111
10. Snarl words are _____; purr words are

   _____.
   Answer: highly negative; highly positive

Essay

Write your answer in the space provided or on a separate sheet of paper.

Pages: 132-133
1. Give three examples of sexist language. Revise them using inclusive language.
   Answer: Reference: p. 132-133

Pages: 121-123

2. How can you avoid confusing facts and inferences?
   Answer: Recognize that inferences may be wrong
            Use tentative language
            Be prepared to be proved wrong

Pages: 110-117

3. List the principles of meaning. How can following these principles improve communication?
   Answer: Look for meaning in people, not in words.
            Meanings depend on context.
            Meanings are packaged.
            Meanings are denotative and connotative

Chapter 6   Nonverbal Messages

Multiple-Choice

Choose the one alternative that best completes the statement or answers the question.

Pages: 145
1. According to the facial feedback hypothesis,
    A) facial movements indicate eight emotions
    B) we cover up sadness so as not to depress others
    C) facial expression directly translates words or phrases
    D) facial expression influences the level of physiological arousal
    Answer: D

Pages: 162
2. With a future time orientation, you would:
    A) relive old times
    B) deny luxuries today in order to save for the future
    C) pay particular reverence for the past
    D) live for today, not for tomorrow
    Answer: B

Pages: 150
3. People of equal status
    A) discuss personal subjects
    B) have dilated pupils when they interact
    C) maintain shorter distances between them than people of unequal status
    D) move less than people of unequal status
    E) pause more than people of unequal status
    Answer: C

Pages: 160
4. Silence
    A) functions differently from other forms of nonverbal communication
    B) is most common between people of unequal status
    C) is used differently in different cultures
    D) does not communicate emotions
    Answer: C

Pages: 148
5. "Proxemics" is:
   A) the study of space communication
   B) the study of body communication
   C) the study of touch communication
   D) the study of time communication
   Answer: A

Pages: 156
6. "Haptics" is:
   A) the study of eye communication
   B) the study of body communication
   C) the study of facial communication
   D) the study of touch communication
   Answer: D

Pages: 387
7. "Kinesics" is:
   A) the study of touch communication
   B) the study of space communication
   C) the study of time communication
   D) the study of body communication
   Answer: D

Pages: 143
8. Nonverbal messages which convey emotional meanings are:
   A) emblems
   B) regulators
   C) adaptors
   D) illustrators
   E) affect displays
   Answer: E

9. Nonverbal messages with direct translations are:
   A) illustrators
   B) emblems
   C) adaptors
   D) affect displays
   E) regulators
   Answer: B

10. Nonverbal messages which influence the speaking of another person are:
    A) adaptors
    B) illustrators
    C) regulators
    D) emblems
    E) affect displays
    Answer: C

11. "Primary affect displays" are:
    A) done by elementary-age children
    B) usually in bright, clear colors
    C) relatively pure emotions
    D) emotions we experience at an early age
    Answer: C

12. Color impacts meaning in all of the following ways EXCEPT:
    A) plant growth
    B) respiratory rates
    C) perceptions of packaging
    D) jury decisions
    Answer: A

Pages: 155
13. Space decoration:
   A) is a concern of NASA's
   B) relates to offices but not homes
   C) influences inferences about you
   D) is primarily concerned with size
   Answer: C

Pages: 148
14. "Visual dominance behavior" is:
   A) looking out for the other person
   B) maintaining greater eye contact while listening than speaking
   C) maintaining greater eye contact while speaking than listening
   D) a form of hypnotism
   Answer: C

Pages: 148
15. Looking away while someone nearby is having an argument is an example of:
   A) visual dominance behavior
   B) nonverbal rules
   C) compensating for distance
   D) civil inattention
   Answer: D

Pages: 149
16. Personal distance is from:
   A) 12 - 25 feet
   B) 18 inches to 4 feet
   C) contact to 18 inches
   D) 4 feet to 12 feet
   Answer: B

Pages: 152
17. Leaving a sweater to "save" a chair is an example of:
   A) markers
   B) territoriality
   C) ear markers
   D) territorial encroachment
   Answer: A

Pages: 156
18. The first sense we use is:
    A) smell
    B) taste
    C) hearing
    D) touch
    Answer: D

Pages: 157
19. Scientific studies show that people who avoid touching also:
    A) avoid eating
    B) enjoy hugging
    C) avoid self-disclosure
    D) are more likely to be young women
    Answer: C

Pages: 157
20. Paralanguage is:
    A) verbal and nonverbal
    B) verbal and vocal
    C) vocal and nonverbal
    D) communication about communication
    Answer: C

Pages: 158
21. Belching is an example of:
    A) paralanguage
    B) a lack of communication
    C) disrespect
    D) an example of haptics
    Answer: A

Pages: 158
22. The aspect of paralanguage which has received the most attention is:
    A) one-way communication
    B) rate of speech
    C) to request a turn as speaker
    D) pitch of speech
    Answer: B

Pages: 158
23. Which sentence conveys the meaning that I think someone besides you stole the money?
    A) I did not SAY you stole the money.
    B) I did not say YOU stole the money.
    C) I did not say you STOLE the money.
    D) I did not say you stole the MONEY.
    Answer: B

Pages: 162-164
24. Future income is positively related to:
    A) present-orientation
    B) hedonism
    C) future-orientation
    D) time sensitivity
    Answer: C

True-False

Write T if the statement is true and F if the statement is false.

Pages: 143
1. A regulating message is one which gives instructions and rules.
   Answer: False

2. Nonverbal behavior always communicates.
   Answer: True

Pages: 145
3. Subjects who exaggerate their facial expressions how higher physiological arousal than those who suppress expressions.
   Answer: True

Pages: 146
4. In our culture, the average length of a mutual gaze is 5.1 seconds.
   Answer: False

Pages: 143
5. Affect displays deal with the effects of nonverbal communication.
   Answer: False

Pages: 146
6. In our culture, there are rather strict rules for the appropriate length of eye contact.
   Answer: True

Pages: 149
7. Social distance is from 12 to 25 feet.
   Answer: False

Pages: 152
8. Initials on a shirt or attache' case are examples of markers.
   Answer: True

Pages: 158-159
9. Listeners can judge emotional states of speakers just from their vocal expression.
   Answer: True

Pages: 164
10. Present-oriented people have greater incomes than future-oriented people.
    Answer: False

Short Answer

Write the word or phrase that best completes each statement or answers the question.

Pages: 145
1. According to the facial feedback hypothesis, your facial expression influences your level of _____.
   Answer: physiological arousal

Pages: 164
2. The time orientation you develop depends on your _____ class.
   Answer: socioeconomic

Pages: 153
3. Messages created or arranged by human hands are _____ messages.
   Answer: artifactual

Pages: 143
4. Affect displays are _____ movements that convey _____ meaning.
   Answer: facial, emotional

Pages: 144
5. Learning to hide certain emotions and to emphasize others are examples of
   _____ techniques.
   Answer: facial management

Pages: 148
6. Eye communication serves three major functions:
   Answer: to seek feedback
           to inform the other of open communication channels
           to signal the nature of the relationship

Pages: 148
7. Our pupils _____ when we are interested in something.
   Answer: enlarge

Pages: 149-150
8. The four distances that define relationships are:
   Answer: intimate, personal, social, public

Pages: 156
9. Touching varies greatly from one _____ to another.
   Answer: culture

Pages: 162
10. Formal time units are _____.
    Answer: arbitrary

Essay

Write your answer in the space provided or on a separate sheet of paper.

Pages: 142
1. How should one go about studying nonverbal communication? Give four suggestions with an example of each.
   Answer: Reference: pp. 142

Pages: 142-167
2. Describe how the various forms of nonverbal communicate interact. Use an example or a situation to illustrate this.
   Answer: Reference: pp. 142-167

Pages: 149-150
3. Give an example of each of the four spatial distances being used to communicate.
   Answer: Reference: pp. 149-150

Chapter 7   Emotional Messages

Multiple-Choice

Choose the one alternative that best completes the statement or answers the question.

Pages: 189-190
1. I-messages:
    A) are ego-centric
    B) focus the discussion on yourself
    C) avoid cliches
    D) signal a willingness to be responsible for your feelings
    Answer: D

Pages: 183
2. The tendency to frown on any kind of emotional expression has been called:
    A) macho
    B) the cowboy syndrome
    C) denial
    D) fear of exposing weakness
    Answer: B

Pages: 183-186
3. The three obstacles to effective emotional expression include all EXCEPT:
    A) destructive beliefs
    B) inadequate interpersonal skills
    C) fear of exposing weakness
    D) societal rules
    Answer: A

Pages: 185
4. The most important obstacle to effectively communicating emotions is:
    A) fear of exposing weakness
    B) destructive beliefs
    C) lack of interpersonal skills
    D) societal rules
    Answer: C

Pages: 193

5. "You can't cry now; you have to set an example," is an example of a statement that is:
   A) a destructive belief
   B) an affirming belief
   C) good advice
   D) disconfirming
   Answer: D

Pages: 193

6. Which of the following statements would be an example of confirming the other person and their feelings?
   A) Keep that stiff upper lip; no one would know you are in pain.
   B) I've gone through what you are experiencing; I know what you feel.
   C) You must be in such pain.
   D) Just be thankful that it isn't any worse.
   Answer: C

Pages: 189

7. When you anchor your feelings to the present, you
   A) fall into the trap of believing negative statements
   B) limit your references to the here and now
   C) demonstrate empathy
   D) own your own feelings
   Answer: B

Pages: 188

8. Perhaps the most important guideline for effective emotional expressions is:
   A) anchor your feelings to the present
   B) identify the reasons for your feelings
   C) own your own feelings
   D) describe your feelings accurately
   Answer: C

Pages: 189-190
9. "When you neglect to introduce me to your friends, I feel like I don't matter," is an example of a statement that is:
    A) owning your own feelings
    B) affirming
    C) empathic
    D) anchored to the present
    Answer: A

Pages: 189
10. "You make me feel like I don't belong," is an example of a statement that is:
    A) affirming
    B) disconfirming
    C) anchored to the present
    D) blaming the other person
    Answer: D

Pages: 174
11. Communicating emotions is difficult because:
    A) we feel inadequate
    B) there are few words to describe emotions
    C) our thinking is confused when we are emotional
    D) emotional expression is damaging to relationships
    Answer: C

Pages: 175-176
12. The emotion we feel has three components:
    A) mind, culture, expression
    B) mind, body, culture
    C) culture, body, awareness
    D) interpretation, body, mind
    E) interpretation, expression, culture
    Answer: B

Pages: 175-176
13. The mental part of our emotional experience involves all EXCEPT:
    A) interpretations
    B) evaluations
    C) easily observable reactions
    D) appraisals
    Answer: C

Pages: 175
14. The emotions we feel seem due in large part to:
    A) the immediate stimulus
    B) the interpretations we give to events
    C) physiology
    D) our own decisions to feel
    Answer: B

Pages: 188
15. Which of the following statements is an example of describing feelings?
    A) I feel hurt that he didn't call.
    B) He is a bum.
    C) I can't count on him.
    D) Why does this always happen to me?!
    Answer: A

Pages: 189
16. Which of the following statements is an example of owning feelings?
    A) He made me feel bad.
    B) The cat's dying made me feel black and blue inside.
    C) I'll never forgive her.
    D) I get scared and hurt when you don't call me.
    Answer: D

Pages: 178
17. The commonsense view of emotions says:
    A) an event occurs, we respond physiologically, we experience an emotion
    B) an event occurs, we experience an emotion, we respond physiologically
    C) an event occurs, we respond physiologically, we interpret this arousal. we experience the emotion
    D) we experience the emotion, we respond physiologically, we interpret this arousal
    Answer: B

Pages: 178
18. The cognitive-labeling theory of emotions says:
    A) an event occurs, we respond physiologically, we interpret this arousal, we experience the emotion
    B) an event occurs, we respond physiologically, we experience an emotion
    C) we respond physiologically, we experience an emotion, an event occurs
    D) an event occurs, we experience an emotion, we respond physiologically
    Answer: A

Pages: 179
19. The James-Lange theory of emotions says:
    A) an event occurs, we experience an emotion, we respond physiologically
    B) we experience an emotion, we respond physiologically, we interpret the arousal
    C) an event occurs, we respond physiologically, we interpret this arousal, we experience the emotion
    D) an event occurs, we respond physiologically, we experience an emotion
    Answer: D

Pages: 180
20. You decide to act calmly even though you are angry. This is an example of:
    A) emotions
    B) emotional expression
    C) emotional behavior
    D) all of the above
    Answer: C

Pages: 175

21. What is the most obvious aspect of our emotional experience?
    A) our evaluations
    B) our cultural environment
    C) our bodily reactions
    D) our interpretations
    Answer: C

Pages: 181

22. A positive way to let out your emotions at work is:
    A) Let your emotions churn in your head
    B) Immediately express your feelings to let off steam
    C) Collect all of the instances which upset you to discuss at once
    D) Write your feelings on paper -- and then destroy it
    Answer: D

Pages: 174

23. Communicating emotionally is difficult for all of the following reasons EXCEPT:
    A) we've not been taught how to communicate emotions
    B) out emotions confuse our thinking
    C) we care less about our emotions than our thinking
    D) there are few effective models
    Answer: C

Pages: 177

24. Basic emotions are:
    A) related to our base selves
    B) primary emotions
    C) a blend of happy and sad emotions
    D) unrelated to facial expression
    Answer: B

Pages: 180

25. Emotional expression is all EXCEPT:
    A) difficult
    B) essential in interpersonal relationships
    C) uncontrollable behavior
    D) the way you choose to communicate feelings
    Answer: C

True-False

Write T if the statement is true and F if the statement is false.

Pages: 175-176
1. Emotion involves three components: bodily reactions, mental evaluations, and situations.
   Answer: False

Pages: 175-176
2. Our evaluations of what happens have a greater impact on our feelings than what actually happens.
   Answer: True

Pages: 176
3. Sexually stereotyped behavior is an example of the impact of culture on emotional expression.
   Answer: True

Pages: 182
4. Be assertive about your beliefs and responsive to the other person's perspective.
   Answer: True

Pages: 185
5. Failing to express negative feelings will probably not help your relationships.
   Answer: True

Pages: 177
6. According to Robert Plutchik, there are ten basic emotions.
   Answer: False

Pages: 178
7. The James-Lange theory of emotions says that we respond physiologically to our perception of an emotion.
   Answer: False

Pages: 178

8. The cognitive-labeling theory of emotions says that we experience emotions after we interpret our physiological reactions.
Answer: True

Pages: 180

9. "Emotional expressions" and "emotional behavior" are terms which both refer to the way we act out the emotions we feel.
Answer: False

Pages: 180

10. We are clearly in control of the ways in which we express our emotions.
Answer: True

Short Answer

Write the word or phrase that best completes each statement or answers the question.

Pages: 175-176

1. The three components of emotions include _____, _____ and
_____.
Answer: body, mind, culture

Pages: 175

2. The emotions we feel seem due in large part to the _____ we give to events.
Answer: interpretations or meanings

Pages: 176

3. The _____ we live in gives us a framework for interpreting the emotions of others and expressing our own.
Answer: culture

Pages: 191

4. When responding to the emotions of others, try to see the situation from the _____ of the speaker.
Answer: point of view

Pages: 191
5. Communicating your feelings is only half the process; the other half is
   _____ and _____ to the feelings of others.
   Answer: listening and responding

Pages: 177
6. According to Robert Plutchik, the basic emotions include: joy, acceptance, _____,
   _____, _____, disgust, anticipation, and _____.
   Answer: fear, surprise, sadness, anger

Pages: 189
7. The opposite of owning your own feelings is _____.
   Answer: blaming the other person

Pages: 186-190
8. Before describing your emotions, focus on these preliminary tasks:
   Answer: understand your emotions, decide whether you wish to express your feelings, and
            assess your communication options

Pages: 193
9. Give a grieving person _____ to grieve.
   Answer: permission

Pages: 189
10. _____ show that you take responsibility for your own emotions.
    Answer: I-messages

Essay

Write your answer in the space provided or on a separate sheet of paper.

Pages: 174-176
1. Give an example of each of the three components of emotion.
   Answer: body, mind, culture

Pages: 178

2. Contrast the three theories of emotional arousal. Present a logical argument in favor of the one you prefer.

   Answer: Commonsense theory
   James-Lange theory
   Cognitive-labeling theory

Pages: 186-190

3. List four suggestions for expressing emotions effectively. Give an example of each.

   Answer: understand your emotions
   decide if you wish to express your feelings
   assess your communication options
   describe your feelings

Chapter 8   Conversation Messages

Multiple-Choice

Choose the one alternative that best completes the statement or answers the question.

Pages: 204
1. "You'll probably think I'm crazy, but ..." is an example of:
    A) hedging
    B) sin license
    C) cognitive disclaimer
    D) credentialing
    Answer: C

Pages: 204
2. "I'm no physical therapist, but ..." is an example of:
    A) hedging
    B) credentialing
    C) cognitive disclaimer
    D) appeal for suspension of judgment
    Answer: A

Pages: 218
3. "Let's get together next week," is an example of:
    A) asking for closure
    B) expressing your enjoyment with the conversation
    C) referring to future interaction
    D) summarizing the conversation
    Answer: C

Pages: 217
4. Three classes of excuses are:
    A) alibi; denial; yes, but
    B) I didn't do it; yes, but; it wasn't so bad
    C) yes, but; it wasn't so bad; I couldn't help it
    D) alibi, I didn't do it; stonewall
    Answer: B

Pages: 217
5. Denial of having done what one is accused of is an example of what kind of excuse?
   A) yes, but
   B) it wasn't so bad
   C) I didn't do it
   D) all of the above
   Answer: C

Pages: 217
6. Claiming that you couldn't help doing something is an example of which type of excuse?
   A) it wasn't so bad
   B) yes, but
   C) I didn't do it
   D) none of the above
   Answer: B

Pages: 224
7. A willingness to self-disclose is an example of:
   A) supportiveness
   B) openness
   C) empathy
   D) descriptiveness
   Answer: B

Pages: 228
8. Taking responsibility for one's thoughts and feelings, encouraging openness in others, and providing appropriate feedback are characteristics of:
   A) other-orientation
   B) immediacy
   C) expressiveness
   D) high self-monitoring
   Answer: C

Pages: 227
9. The creation of a sense of togetherness relates to:
   A) confirmation
   B) expressiveness
   C) immediacy
   D) interaction management
   Answer: C

Pages: 227
10. Reinforcing and complimenting the other person is an example of:
    A) allness
    B) confirmation
    C) disconfirmation
    D) immediacy
    Answer: D

Pages: 226
11. Which of the following messages is an example of positive stroking?
    A) saying "I love you" and forgetting your birthday
    B) repeatedly cancelling appointments with you to discuss our top priorities
    C) telling your child that you cancelled a business appointment to make it to the school open house
    D) arriving late for an evening with best friends
    E) telling friends you miss them terribly but not writing to them
    Answer: C

Pages: 228
12. High self-monitors
    A) adjust their behavior in order to produce the most desirable effect
    B) avoid negative criticism
    C) do not attempt to manipulate the impression they make
    D) find it hard to imitate the behavior of other people
    Answer: A

Pages: 230

13. An other-oriented communicator
    A) frequently uses negative criticism
    B) acknowledges the legitimacy of others' feelings
    C) is willing to self-disclose
    D) uses "requests for honest criticism" in order to get praise or approval
    Answer: B

Pages: 202

14. The process of conversation involves five steps. They are:
    A) opening, closing, middle, business, transitions
    B) closing, feedback, business, feedforward, opening
    C) feedforward, feedforward, business, transitions, closing
    D) opening, feedforward, business, closing, follow-up
    Answer: B

Pages: 204

15. Which of the following is NOT an example of a <u>disclaimer</u>?
    A) hedging
    B) sin license
    C) altercasting
    D) credentialing
    Answer: C

Pages: 209

16. Which of the following is a violation which could damage an entire conversation?
    A) warning a person that you have bad news for them
    B) spending time to be sure that all participants know each other
    C) spending time closing the conversation by paraphrasing what was decided
    D) using a insensitive opening
    Answer: D

Pages: 218

17. The four conversational metaskills are:
    A) flexibility, metacommunicational ability, cultural sensitivity, mindfulness
    B) flexibility, altercasting, high self-monitoring, cultural sensitivity
    C) high self-monitoring, expressiveness, openness, metacommunicaitonal ability
    D) mindfulness, openness, altercasting, credentialing
    Answer: A

Pages: 200

18. The defining feature of conversation is:
    A) enjoyment
    B) accomplishing business
    C) exchanging speaker and listener roles
    D) establishing an effective monologue
    Answer: C

Pages: 214

19. A speaker audibly inhaling breath and avoiding eye contact is signalling:
    A) it is someone else's turn to speak
    B) the conversation is coming to a close
    C) the speaker is about to open a new topic
    D) the speaker does not want to give up the floor
    Answer: D

Pages: 214-215

20. Saying "um" and beginning to gesture is an example of
    A) turn-yielding cue
    B) turn-requesting cue
    C) turn-maintaining cue
    D) backchanneling cue
    Answer: B

Pages: 216

21. If you discover in a conversation that you said something that will lead to disapproval, you can seek to correct it. What strategy would you use?
    A) altercasting
    B) feedforward
    C) excuses
    D) credentialing
    Answer: C

217

Pages: 218
22. Closing a conversation:
    A) is almost as difficult as opening one
    B) is impolite
    C) should be initiated by the speaker
    D) should be the longest part of the conversation
    Answer: A

Pages: 230
23. Having an other-orientation means:
    A) your rights may be denied
    B) you should just sit quietly and let the interaction be directed by other
    C) you are internationally minded
    D) the ability to communicate interest and attentiveness to the other
    Answer: D

Pages: 216-217
24. Excuses allow all of the following EXCEPT:
    A) lessening the negative impact of the message
    B) justifying your poor performance
    C) maintaining interpersonal relationships
    D) reversing previous communication
    Answer: D

True-False

Write T if the statement is true and F if the statement is false.

Pages: 227
1. Immediacy is communication between two people in close proximity.
    Answer: False

Pages: 206-208
2. Mindfulness is a perfect example of feedback.
    Answer: False

Pages: 208

3. Generally, the most effective feedback is that which is most immediate.
   Answer: True

Pages: 210

4. Self references are a poor way of opening a conversation.
   Answer: False

Pages: 212

5. Disclose intimate information about yourself early in a conversation in order to establish rapport.
   Answer: False

Pages: 214

6. One way a speaker prevents the listener from speaking is by vocalizing pauses (er, um).
   Answer: True

Pages: 212

7. The "thought-completer" knows ecxactly what you are going to say and says it for you.
   Answer: True

Pages: 210

8. A culturally based conversational rule in the US is to talk about irrelevancies in order to establish rapport.
   Answer: False

Pages: 223

9. Metacommunication is only effective if you get beyond talk about talk to talk about the problem.
   Answer: True

Pages: 227

10. Someone who is effective at interaction management is able to control the conversation by holding on to the floor.
    Answer: False

Short Answer

Write the word or phrase that best completes each statement or answers the question.

Pages: 228
1. Self-monitoring is the _____ of the image you project to others.
   Answer: manipulation

Pages: 205
2. By using a _____, we try to ensure that our message will be understood as we wish it to be.
   Answer: disclaimer

Pages: 225
3. To feel as the other person feels is _____.
   Answer: empathy

Pages: 227
4. The creation of a sense of togetherness is _____.
   Answer: immediacy

Pages: 227
5. In effective _____, neither person feels ignored or on stage.
   Answer: interaction management

Pages: 228
6. _____ are not concerned with the image they present to others.
   Answer: low self-monitors

Pages: 230
7. _____ is the ability to communicate attentiveness and interest in the other person and in what is being said.
   Answer: other-orientation

Pages: 228
8. The expressive speaker communicates genuine _____ in the interpersonal interaction.
   Answer: involvement

Pages: 206
9. <u>Business</u> is a good term for this stage of the conversation because it emphasizes that most conversations are _____.
    Answer: goal-directed

Pages: 202
10. Greetings can be _____ or _____.
    Answer: verbal, nonverbal

Pages: 210
11. Conversational violations may have significant consequences because people are not aware of the rules and hence do not see violations as simply _____.
    Answer: cultural differences

Essay

Write your answer in the space provided or on a separate sheet of paper.

Pages: 227
1. How can you create a sense of immediacy with language?
    Answer: maintain physical closeness
            focus on the other person's remarks
            reinforce, reward, or compliment the other person
            maintain appropriate eye contact

Pages: 217
2. What kinds of situations seem to encourage excuse-making? Give examples of three types of excuses.
    Answer: Situations in which we have done something, or are accused of doing something, that will be perceived negatively
            1) I didn't do it, 2) It wasn't so bad, 3) Yes, but

Pages: 226
3. Analyze a situation in which empathy was demonstrated. Identify at least four specific strategies.
    Answer: self-disclose
    maintain eye contact
    avoid judgment
    use reinforcing comments
    demonstrate interest with eye contact, physical closeness, leaning forward, etc.

Pages: 202
4. Make plans for an upcoming conversation following all five steps in the process. What will you do at each step; what do you predict the other person will do?
    Answer: opening; feedforward; business; feedback; closing

Chapter 9   Interpersonal Communication and Culture

Multiple-Choice

Choose the one alternative that best completes the statement or answers the question.

Pages: 239
1. One reason intercultural communication is more important today than before is:
   A) students are learning more languages
   B) space travel will link us all together
   C) immigration to the USA is rapidly increasing
   D) the environment is breaking down
   Answer: C

Pages: 241
2. Culture means all of the following EXCEPT:
   A) a specialized life-style
   B) other cultures are attempting to develop to the extent American culture has
   C) values, beliefs, behavior
   D) language, art, religion
   Answer: B

Pages: 241
3. Enculturation means:
   A) the transmission of culture from one generation to another
   B) processes that modify a person's culture through contact with other cultures
   C) communication between persons of different cultures
   D) all that a social group has produced and developed.
   Answer: A

Pages: 242
4. Intercultural communication means:
   A) the transmission of culture from one generation to another
   B) processes that modify a person's culture through contact with other cultures
   C) communication between persons of different cultures
   D) all that a social group has produced and developed.
   Answer: C

Pages: 241

5. <u>Acculturation</u> means:
   A) the transmission of culture from one generation to another
   B) processes that modify a person's culture through contact with other cultures
   C) communication between persons of different cultures
   D) all that a social group has produced and developed.
   Answer: B

Pages: 243

6. Communication between the United States and Brazil would be an example of:
   A) interethnic communication
   B) international communication
   C) interracial communication
   D) ethnocentric
   Answer: B

Pages: 243

7. Communication between Japanese-Americans and Greek-Americans is an example of:
   A) interethnic communication
   B) international communication
   C) interracial communication
   D) ethnocentric
   Answer: A

Pages: 243

8. Communication between Hispanics and Orientals is an example of:
   A) interethnic communication
   B) international communication
   C) interracial communication
   D) ethnocentric
   Answer: C

Pages: 251

9. An example of ethnocentrism is:
   A) civil war
   B) ignoring differences
   C) behaving mindlessly
   D) teaching children about their heritage
   Answer: A

Pages: 252
10. An example of mindlessness is:
    A) forgetting where you left your key
    B) failing a test
    C) ignoring differences among cultures
    D) being afraid to touch a mongoloid child
    Answer: D

Pages: 252
11. In a mindful state,
    A) we are non-rational
    B) we resort to a critical-thinking mode
    C) we recognize other cultures are inferior
    D) we ignore barriers and gateways to intercultural communication
    Answer: B

Pages: 254
12. Knowing some of the barriers to intercultural communication
    A) is depressing
    B) may help you avoid them
    C) will hamper intercultural communication
    D) can only happen after living in other cultures
    Answer: B

Pages: 247
13. A high-context culture is also
    A) a collectivist culture
    B) an individualistic culture
    C) an ethnocentric culture
    D) a competitive culture
    Answer: A

Pages: 257
14. The nonverbal gesture of waving
    A) is universal across cultures
    B) was created in the United States
    C) means you know a secret in Scotland
    D) is insulting in Greece
    Answer: D

Pages: 260
15. Our behaviors
    A) are innate
    B) are natural
    C) are learned
    D) are evaluative
    Answer: C

Pages: 248-251
16. According to the article on Corporate Cultures, behavior norms are all of the following EXCEPT:
    A) visible patterns of behavior
    B) are clearly described in policy guidelines
    C) self-reinforcing
    D) "the way we do things around here"
    Answer: B

Pages: 260
17. Which of the following would NOT be appropriate in order to avoid the common barriers:
    A) behave according to Emily Post and you'll be OK
    B) recognize the differences within the group
    C) be aware of cultural rules
    D) avoid negative evaluations
    Answer: A

Pages: 262
18. Being empathetic to someone from another culture means:
    A) sympathizing with their problems
    B) adopt their ways as your own
    C) speak for the person so he/she won't have to struggle with the language
    D) try to see the world from this person's perspective
    Answer: D

Pages: 242
19. The model of intercultural communication in this chapter indicates that:
    A) culture is only a part of our communication experience
    B) intercultural communication is a rare experience
    C) each communicator is a member of a different culture
    D) our daily lives are not impacted by cultural differences unless we live in a foreign country
    Answer: C

Pages: 251
20. Racism, sexism and heterosexism are closely related to
    A) acculturation
    B) ethnocentrism
    C) mindfulness
    D) expressiveness
    Answer: B

True-False

Write T if the statement is true and F if the statement is false.

Pages: 239
1. Intercultural communication is more important and vital today than at any other point in history.
   Answer: True

Pages: 241
2. Culture refers to the finer elements of our lifestyles: art, music, drama, dance.
   Answer: False

Pages: 241-242
3. Enculturation, acculturation, and intercultural are the steps in a model of cross-cultural communication.
   Answer: False

Pages: 243
4. Communication between the sexes is also intercultural.
   Answer: True

Pages: 251
5. We are all a little ethnocentric, tending to see our own culture as superior to that of others.
   Answer: True

Pages: 254
6. When you assume that others are like you, you are implicitly complimenting and affirming them.
   Answer: False

Pages: 258
7. The use of eyes to communicate remains fairly consistent across cultures.
   Answer: False

Pages: 262
8. Good conversational techniques will be of assistance as you work at communicating across cultures.
   Answer: True

Pages: 260
9. Cultural rules and customs are arbitrary and convenient.
   Answer: True

Pages: 260
10. We learn our behaviors from our culture.
    Answer: True

Short Answer

Write the word or phrase that best completes each statement or answers the question.

Pages: 239
1. Three reasons for the rapid increase of intercultural communication today are
   _____, _____, and _____.
   Answer: increased immigration, increase in communication technology, increased travel

Pages: 241

2. _____ includes all that members of a social group have produced and developed.
   Answer: culture

Pages: 242-243

3. You receive messages through _____ imposed by a unique culture.
   Answer: filters

Pages: 242

4. _____ influences every aspect of your communication experience.
   Answer: culture

Pages: 251

5. Ethnocentrism exists on a _____.
   Answer: continuum

Pages: 252

6. Being reluctant to swim after a mental patient had been in the pool is an example of _____.
   Answer: mindlessness

Pages: 254

7. Assuming that all people are similar is an example of _____.
   Answer: ignoring differences

Pages: 246

8. In a low-context culture, most information is stated _____.
   Answer: explicitly

Pages: 260

9. We learn our _____ from our _____.
   Answer: behaviors, culture

Pages: 263

10. Remember the interaction management principle of being sensitive to differences in _____ when in conversation with people of different cultures.
    Answer: turn-taking

Essay

Write your answer in the space provided or on a separate sheet of paper.

Pages: 253
1. Provide an example of each of the five degrees of ethnocentrism.
   Answer: equality
            sensitivity
            indifference
            avoidance
            disparagement

Pages: 260
2. Assume you are a consultant to a businessperson going to do business in a foreign country for the first time. What are primary steps you would recommend in order for that person to avoid the common barriers to intercultural communication.
   Answer: recognize differences between yourself and the culturally different person
            recognize differences exist within any group
            remember meaning is in the person
            be aware of cultural rules
            avoid negative evaluations

Pages: 241
3. Identify something in your own experience which demonstrates enculturation. How has it been impacted by acculturation?
   Answer: Discuss something learned and then changed

Pages: 243
4. How many forms of intercultural communication are available to you on the campus where you are studying?
   Answer: intercultural
            interracial
            interethnic
            inter-religious
            international
            with smaller cultures within the larger one
            with smaller groups and the dominant culture
            between the sexes

230

Chapter 10 Interpersonal Communication and Relationships

Multiple-Choice

Choose the one alternative that best completes the statement or answers the question.

Pages: 300
1. Empathic understanding, fair fighting, reasonableness, openness to change, and self-disclosures are
   A) general principles of effective communication
   B) the steps in attraction theory
   C) affinity-seeking strategies
   D) disengagement strategies
   Answer: A

Pages: 270
2. The most general reason for establishing relationships is:
   A) to increase self-esteem
   B) to gain self-knowledge
   C) to gain stimulation
   D) to maximize pleasure/minimize pain
   E) to lesson loneliness
   Answer: D

Pages: 275
3. When we begin to reveal ourselves to the other person, we are at which stage of a relationship?
   A) contact
   B) intimacy
   C) dissolution
   D) deterioration
   E) involvement
   Answer: E

Pages: 280
4. The theory that love is a game, entertaining and exciting or not at all, is a description of:
A) storge
B) eros
C) manic
D) ludus
E) pragma
Answer: D

Pages: 284-286
5. When a person says something like "Couldn't we discuss this and work something out?", she/he is sending which kind of message?
A) contact
B) closeness
C) distancing
D) repair
E) dissolution
Answer: D

Pages: 286-287
6. Which of the following messages indicates a desire to begin to separate from the relationship?
A) Look, it's not working out.
B) I'm eager to get together again soon.
C) I think we should spend a few weeks apart.
D) Hi, haven't we met before?
E) I'm sorry I was so stubborn.
Answer: C

Pages: 281-282
7. At which phase do individuals begin to share their dissatisfaction and decision to leave with others?
A) contact
B) closeness
C) deterioration
D) repair
E) dissolution
Answer: C

Pages: 275-277

8. Which of the following statements is an example of what might be said during the involvement stage of a relationship?
   A) I'd like to take you to the play we discussed.
   B) You never listen to me.
   C) May I join you?
   D) I love you.
   Answer: A

Pages: 271-273

9. Which statement is an example of the kind of comment made during the contact stage?
   A) Will you marry me?
   B) It's all your fault.
   C) Have I seen you here before?
   D) Goodbye.
   Answer: C

Pages: 281-282

10. Which statement is an example of a deteriorating relationship?
    A) How are you?
    B) I want a divorce.
    C) Let's not date each other exclusively.
    D) Will you go out with me?
    Answer: C

Pages: 290

11. How does movement among the stages of a relationship work?
    A) There is a forward progression through the stages.
    B) If a relationship does not keep moving through the stages, it dies.
    C) The stages always progress from less intense to more intense.
    D) Each stage offers the opportunity to exit the relationship.
    Answer: D

Pages: 297
12. We can describe all relationships:
    A) as uniform in depth
    B) with the concepts of breadth and depth
    C) as moving toward increased intimacy
    D) as a positive force
    Answer: B

Pages: 297-298
13. Which of the following would you NOT do in the process of depenetration?
    A) omit certain topics from communication
    B) reduce the level of self-disclosures
    C) seek to spend more time with the other person
    D) discuss topics in less depth
    Answer: C

Pages: 287
14. If a relationship does end, which of the following would NOT be a good idea?
    A) bolster self-esteem
    B) seek support
    C) avoid sad passivity
    D) look for someone just like the person in the relationship which ended
    Answer: D

Pages: 298
15. Social exchange theory is based on the idea that:
    A) profits = rewards - costs
    B) the ratio of your rewards should be equal to that of your partner's
    C) the breadth and depth of interaction increase during depenetration
    D) you should protect yourself against the costs of any relationship
    Answer: A

Pages: 292-294
16. The four factors which account for the appeal of one person for another are:
    A) proximity, attractiveness, intimacy, similarity
    B) similarity, need-fulfillment, socialization, proximity
    C) proximity, attractiveness, similarity, reinforcement
    D) attractiveness, reinforcement, propinquity, availability
    Answer: C

Pages: 270
17. The most general reason for establishing relationships is:
    A) you learn about yourself
    B) maximize pleasure and minimize pain
    C) stimulation of ideas
    D) loneliness
    Answer: B

Pages: 272
18. At the contact state, which of the following is particularly important?
    A) ability to articulate ideas
    B) opening line
    C) an introduction
    D) physical appearance
    Answer: D

Pages: 277
19. Partners test each other during their relationship with which of the following strategies:
    A) separation
    B) social exchange
    C) equity
    D) social penetration
    Answer: A

Pages: 276
20. Endurance means:
    A) spending long periods of time together
    B) increasing rewards
    C) increasing costs
    D) acting negatively to test the relationship
    Answer: D

Pages: 295
21. An affinity-seeking strategy is:
    A) something people can say or do to get others to like them
    B) a way of disengaging from a relationship
    C) a manipulative strategy
    D) generally ineffective
    Answer: A

Pages: 277
22. A formal marriage illustrates an example of:
    A) physical compatibility
    B) social bonding
    C) interpersonal commitment
    D) social penetration
    Answer: B

Pages: 272
23. Physical appearance is especially important at which stage of a relationship?
    A) intimacy
    B) involvement
    C) dissolution
    D) contact
    E) all of the above
    Answer: D

Pages: 298
24. According to social exchange theory, the most preferred relationships are those which:
    A) happen easily
    B) involve a great deal of similarity
    C) give the greatest rewards with the least pain
    D) have great breadth and depth
    Answer: C

25. The degree to which the inner personality -- the inner core of an individual -- is penetrated in interpersonal interaction:
    A) penetration
    B) depth
    C) breadth
    D) contact
    Answer: B

True-False

Write T if the statement is true and F if the statement is false.

Pages: 270
1. We learn about ourselves largely through contact with others.
    Answer: True

Pages: 280
2. Ludus love consists of extreme highs and extreme lows.
    Answer: False

Pages: 286
3. When we cut the bonds that tie individuals together, we are involved in a deteriorating relationship.
    Answer: False

Pages: 286-287
4. As a relationship dissolves, individuals move from a very private experience to one which gradually includes more people.
    Answer: True

Pages: 288
5. "I'm going away to college; there's no point in not dating others" is an example of justification.
    Answer: True

Pages: 275
6. Establishing and talking about common interests is a characteristic of the Involvement Stage of a relationship.
   Answer: True

Pages: 290-291
7. Relationships almost always move in one direction through the five stages.
   Answer: False

Pages: 297
8. The Social Penetration Theory explains only very intimate relationships.
   Answer: False

Pages: 293
9. People usually marry opposites.
   Answer: False

Pages: 293
10. We date and mate with people who tend to be similar to ourselves in physical attractiveness.
    Answer: True

Short Answer

Write the word or phrase that best completes each statement or answers the question.

Pages: 297
1. Relationships vary in breadth and _____.
   Answer: depth

Pages: 277-278
2. After the involvement stage, we select only a few and enter the stage of _____.
   Answer: intimacy

Pages: 280
3. _____ love is practical and traditional.
   Answer: Pragma

Pages: 280
4. The _____ lover wants marriage, a family, a home.
   Answer: storgic

Pages: 297
5. The theory, _____, describes relationships by the number of topics people talk about and their degree of "personalness."
   Answer: social penetration

Pages: 297
6. When a relationship begins to deteriorate, breadth and depth will reverse themselves, a process called _____.
   Answer: depenetration

Pages: 297
7. The _____ of a relationship refers to the number of topics about which you and your partner talk.
   Answer: breadth

Pages: 293
8. The idea that one dates and mates with those who are similar in physical attractiveness is called _____.
   Answer: the similarity principle

Pages: 293
9. We like people who reward or _____ us.
   Answer: reinforce

Pages: 290
10. Each stage of a relationship offers an opportunity _____.
    Answer: to exit from it

Essay

Write your answer in the space provided or on a separate sheet of paper.

Pages: 271-287
1. What general stages do relationships follow? Give an example of the kind of communication that takes place at each stage.
   Answer: contact - superficial
   involvement - share mutual interest
   intimacy - reveal ourselves
   deterioration - less self-disclosure
   repair - disclose your feelings
   dissolution - stage of goodby

Pages: 270
2. Explain why we develop relationships. Give some examples of affinity-seeking strategies that we use to form relationships.
   Answer: to lessen loneliness
   to gain stimulation
   to gain self-knowledge
   to increase self-esteem
   to maximize please/minimize pain

   Affinity seeking strategies such as: be comfortable, dynamism, facilitate enjoyment, listening, inclusion of other (Table 10.2, p. 280)

Pages: 292-294
3. Explain the four factors that account for our appeal to others and theirs to us.
   Answer: attractiveness
   proximity
   reinforcement
   similarity

Chapter 11   Interpersonal Communication and Conflict

Multiple-Choice

Choose the one alternative that best completes the statement or answers the question.

Pages: 310
1. Relationship conflict is everything EXCEPT:
   A) frequent
   B) often deals with who is in charge
   C) may deal with who can set rules
   D) centers on external people, objects and events
   Answer: D

Pages: 313
2. Identifying both content and relationship issues is one way of:
   A) rejecting a solution
   B) gunnysacking
   C) defining the conflict
   D) beltlining
   Answer: C

Pages: 314
3. Most conflicts can be solved:
   A) in only one way
   B) only if one person gives up
   C) if one person wins and one person loses
   D) in a variety of ways
   Answer: D

Pages: 315
4. Nonnegotiation is all of the following EXCEPT:
   A) steamrolling
   B) a special type of avoidance
   C) a silencer
   D) a refusal to discuss or listen to the other person
   Answer: C

Pages: 319
5. Which of the following is an example of evaluation?
   A) you try to control the behavior of the other person
   B) you-messages
   C) you insist on having the last word
   D) you demonstrate indifference or lack of caring
   Answer: B

Pages: 310
6. An example of a relationship conflict is:
   A) fighting over what to watch on television
   B) arguing over politics
   C) disagreeing over who gets to set the rules
   D) trying to convince a professor to change a grade
   Answer: C

Pages: 315-322
7. Which of the following is NOT a productive conflict strategy?
   A) being direct
   B) fighting actively
   C) being specific
   D) focusing on motives
   Answer: D

Pages: 310
8. An example of <u>content conflict</u> is:
   A) trying to decide who is in charge
   B) disagreement over what to watch on television
   C) arguing that one is not being treated fairly
   D) concern over who can set the rules
   Answer: B

Pages: 314
9. Being a devil's advocate allows you to wear the:
   A) feeling hat
   B) positive benefits hat
   C) negative argument hat
   D) fact hat
   Answer: C

Pages: 314
10. Looking at the upside allows you to wear the:
    A) creative new idea hat
    B) positive benefits hat
    C) negative argument hat
    D) fact hat
    Answer: B

Pages: 314
11. Finding new ways to address the problem allows you to wear the:
    A) feeling hat
    B) control of thinking hat
    C) creative new idea hat
    D) fact hat
    Answer: C

Pages: 314
12. Focusing on emotions and intuitions allows you to wear the:
    A) feeling hat
    B) negative argument hat
    C) creative new idea hat
    D) fact hat
    Answer: A

Pages: 314
13. Focusing on data and figures allows you to wear the:
    A) positive benefits hat
    B) negative argument hat
    C) control of thinking hat
    D) fact hat
    Answer: D

Pages: 315
14. Nonnegotiation is a form of:
    A) fighting actively
    B) avoidance
    C) force
    D) present focus
    Answer: B

Pages: 318
15. The only real alternative to force is:
    A) empathy
    B) love
    C) talk
    D) personal rejection
    Answer: C

Pages: 321-322
16. The aim of a relationship conflict, according to the text, is:
    A) to resolve a problem and strengthen the relationship
    B) to win and have your opponent lose
    C) to save the relationship at all costs
    D) to hurt your opponent before you are hurt
    Answer: A

Pages: 322
17. <u>Verbal aggressiveness</u> is all of the following EXCEPT:
    A) disconfirmation
    B) winning by inflicting psychological pain
    C) attacking the other's self concept
    D) willingness to argue for a point of view
    Answer: D

Pages: 324
18. Someone who sees arguments as exciting and is willing to state their position on controversial topics and argue against the positions of others is:
    A) verbally aggressive
    B) a high scorer on argumentativeness
    C) a moderate aggressive
    D) a low argumentative
    Answer: B

Pages: 326
19. A truly argumentative person will:
    A) humiliate the other person
    B) try to prevent arguments
    C) express interest in the other person;s point of view
    D) seek to win at all costs
    Answer: C

Pages: 330
20. Before a fight, you should:
    A) leave the room
    B) bring in additional people on your side
    C) be sure you are each ready to fight
    D) pull no punches
    Answer: C

Pages: 332
21. After the fight,
    A) reward and cherish the other person
    B) avoid the other person
    C) punish the other person
    D) forget it ever happened
    Answer: A

Pages: 310
22. If two people in a relationship fight, it means:
    A) their relationship is a bad one
    B) they are normal
    C) they are being petty
    D) one will lose and one will win
    Answer: B

Pages: 310
23. The thing that really creates a problem is:
    A) revealing your negative side
    B) fighting
    C) being conflict-free
    D) the way a conflict is dealt with
    Answer: D

Pages: 310
24. One of the positive things about conflict is:
    A) there is a clear winner
    B) it forces individuals to examine a problem
    C) there is a clear winner
    D) you can close yourself off from the other individual
    Answer: B

Pages: 313
25. Which of the following is an example of defining the problem in specific terms?
    A) my wife is cold and unfeeling
    B) my husband doesn't really care about the kids
    C) my wife hasn't given me a compliment in six months
    D) he cares more about his work than about me
    Answer: C

True-False

Write T if the statement is true and F if the statement is false.

Pages: 310
1. In a truly good relationship there will be no conflict.
   Answer: False

Pages: 318
2. An unproductive method of dealing with conflict experienced by over 50% of single and married couples involves physical force.
   Answer: True

Pages: 310
3. It is not conflict that creates problems, but the ways in which people deal with it.
   Answer: True

Pages: 313
4. Conflict defined in the abstract is easier to deal with than one which is detailed.
   Answer: False

Pages: 315
5. Active fighting is a negative conflict management strategy.
Answer: False

Pages: 320
6. The best alternative to blame is empathy.
Answer: True

Pages: 321
7. <u>Beltlining</u> a problem means keeping it within limits.
Answer: False

Pages: 322
8. Verbal aggressiveness is the opposite of confirmation.
Answer: True

Pages: 324
9. Argumentativeness leads to unproductive conflict strategies.
Answer: False

Pages: 332
10. After a fight, you should cherish the other person.
Answer: True

Short Answer

Write the word or phrase that best completes each statement or answers the question.

Pages: 318
1. Perhaps the most common unproductive method of dealing with conflict involves _____.
Answer: physical force

Pages: 315
2. A special kind of nonnegotiation is called _____.
Answer: steamrolling

Pages: 321-322
3. The aim of a relationship conflict is to _____ and _____.
   Answer: resolve a problem; strengthen the relationship

Pages: 318
4. Rape is one form of _____.
   Answer: relational force

Pages: 320
5. The best alternative to _____ is empathy.
   Answer: blame

Pages: 321
6. Storing up grievances so that you may unload them during a fight is called
   _____.
   Answer: gunnysacking

Pages: 320
7. The person who appears to know it all is likely to set up a _____ climate.
   Answer: defensive

Pages: 324
8. Argumentativeness is a quality to be _____ rather than _____.
   Answer: cultivated, avoided

Pages: 326
9. The low argumentative tries to _____ arguments.
   Answer: prevent

Pages: 330-332
10. In order for conflict to be truly productive, you need to consider a few strategies both
    _____ and _____ the conflict itself.
    Answer: before, after

Essay

Write your answer in the space provided or on a separate sheet of paper.

Pages: 315-330

1. Contrast productive conflict strategies with unproductive conflict strategies.
   Answer: Discussion of productive strategies should include fight above the belt, fight actively, take responsibility for your thoughts and feelings, be direct and specific, use humor for relief and not ridicule. Discussion of unproductive strategies should include avoidance and nonnegotiation, force, blame, silencers, gunnysacking, manipulation, and personal rejection.

Pages: 312-315

2. The five steps of the conflict model are: _____, _____, _____, _____, and _____
   Answer: define the conflict, examine possible solutions, test the solution, evaluate the solution, accept or reject the solution

Pages: 310-311

3. Give an example of a conflict you experienced which had positive outcomes.
   Answer: forces individuals to examine the problem and work toward a potential solution, enables individuals to state what they want (and sometimes get it), prevents hostilities and resentments from festering

Chapter 12   Interpersonal Communication and Power

Multiple-Choice

Choose the one alternative that best completes the statement or answers the question.

Pages: 339
1. When you feel good about yourself, all of the following are true EXCEPT:
   A) you function better in school
   B) you act like a success
   C) you perform better in general
   D) you are more likely to act like a failure
   Answer: D

Pages: 340-341
2. All of the following are self-destructive beliefs EXCEPT:
   A) I can't do that.
   B) I've never done it before, but I'll try.
   C) They're all snobs, anyway.
   D) You love my brother more than you do me.
   Answer: B

Pages: 342
3. All of the following are self-affirming phrases EXCEPT:
   A) It's not my fault that I'm always the victim.
   B) I always do my best.
   C) I feel good doing the things I'm skilled at.
   D) I am a lovable person.
   Answer: A

Pages: 342
4. In the "just-world hypothesis," all of the following are true EXCEPT:
   A) good people are rewarded - they succeed
   B) bad people are punished - they fail
   C) if you fail, it is probably because of inadequate skills
   D) people get what they deserve
   Answer: C

Pages: 348
5. Some examples of uncertainty expressions include all of the following EXCEPT:
   A) Maybe we could go there later.
   B) I guess I'd like to go.
   C) That's a good book, I think.
   D) That looks pretty good.
   Answer: D

Pages: 342
6. Feeling that you must succeed all the time
   A) leads to success
   B) can only result in disillusionment
   C) will cause you to be a failure
   D) points out an inherent flaw in your character
   Answer: B

Pages: 343
7. Power does all of the following EXCEPT:
   A) permeates all our relationships
   B) influences our employment
   C) enables someone to control the behaviors of someone else
   D) maintains itself at a constant level
   Answer: D

Pages: 355
8. Tactics that influence others to do what you want them to do are called:
   A) explanatory style
   B) power plays
   C) compliance-gaining strategies
   D) unethical
   Answer: C

Pages: 349
9. In the power play, "Nobody Upstairs,"
   A) the person refuses to acknowledge your request
   B) allows you to express your feelings
   C) someone does something for you and expects something in return
   D) you state a cooperative response you can live with
   Answer: A

Pages: 349-350
10. A three-part management strategy for power plays consists of:
    A) Use a metaphor, describe the behavior you object to, state a cooperative response
    B) express your feelings, describe the behavior you object to, explain what you want done by the other person
    C) express your feelings, describe the behavior you object to, state a cooperative response you can both live with
    D) Express your feelings, utilize verbal and nonverbal communication, state a cooperative response
    Answer: C

Pages: 350
11. The power play, "You Owe Me," consists of all the following EXCEPT:
    A) a person does something for you and then demands something in return
    B) puts you in the position of owing someone something
    C) gives the chance to ignore someone socially
    D) allows you to put someone down
    Answer: A

Pages: 343-349
12. Power is all of the following EXCEPT:
    A) a way of life
    B) separate and distinct from general behavior and attitude
    C) used in a variety of ways
    D) an integral part of interpersonal communication
    Answer: B

Pages: 349
13. A response to neutralize power plays involves the following:
    A) describe the behavior to which you object
    B) use aggressiveness, record your behaviors, analyze your behaviors
    C) treat the power play as isolated and object to it
    D) ignore the behavior
    Answer: C

Pages: 356
14. When someone casts you in the role of the "bad" person, they are using:
    A) negative esteem
    B) negative altercasting
    C) moral appeals
    D) threat
    Answer: B

Pages: 356
15. When someone is helpful and friendly in order to get you in a mood to comply, the strategy being used is:
    A) promise
    B) positive altercasting
    C) positive esteem
    D) liking
    Answer: D

Pages: 359
16. Generalized nonassertive people
    A) are extremely sensitive to other's criticisms of their own behavior
    B) are timid, reserved and unable to assert their rights
    C) are fully in charge of themselves in interpersonal relationships
    D) provide frank and open expressions of their feelings
    Answer: B

Pages: 359
17. Generally aggressive people
    A) are aggressive only under certain conditions
    B) act in their own best interests without stepping on others
    C) take over regardless of what is going on
    D) are inhibited and emotionally unresponsive
    Answer: C

Pages: 359
18. Assertive people
   A) exercise their own rights without denying the rights of others
   B) often get into arguments with others
   C) do what others tell them to do without questioning
   D) think little of the opinions, values or beliefs of others
   Answer: A

Pages: 359-360
19. People who are open, not anxious, contentious, and not intimidated are:
   A) aggressive
   B) assertive
   C) nonassertive
   D) nervous about their communication style
   Answer: B

Pages: 356
20. Asking someone to comply because of past favors is an example of:
   A) threat
   B) pre-giving
   C) moral appeals
   D) debt
   Answer: D

Pages: 362
21. The most difficult but important step in becoming more assertive is to
   A) analyze assertive behavior of others
   B) rehearse assertive behaviors
   C) do it
   D) analyze your own behaviors
   Answer: C

Pages: 359
22. Situational nonasssertiveness refers to:
   A) an inability to assert ones rights regardless of the situation
   B) a lack of assertiveness only in certain situations
   C) the attempt to take over in certain situations
   D) requesting permission for doing what is their right
   Answer: B

Pages: 348
23. An example of a tag question is
    A) Would you like to go to the game?
    B) I've never played tag. Have you?
    C) Have you ever played tag?
    D) He's the strongest member of the team, don't you think?
    Answer: D

Pages: 348
24. An example of uncertainty expressions is:
    A) I guess it's a good idea.
    B) I like it, you know.
    C) She's a tried and true friend.
    D) Really, this was the absolute greatest.
    Answer: A

Pages: 356
25. An example of positive altercasting is:
    A) People will think highly of you when go to the opera with me.
    B) A really cultured person would go to the opera with me.
    C) If you don't go to the opera, you'll just grow into a clod.
    D) I'll go to the ball game with you if you will go to the opera with me.
    Answer: B

True-False

Write T if the statement is true and F if the statement is false.

Pages: 339
1. When you think like a success, you are likely to fall on your face.
   Answer: False

Pages: 342
2. In order to be a success, you must succeed in everything you do.
   Answer: False

Pages: 343
3. Power permeates all our interpersonal relationships.
Answer: True

Pages: 343-344
4. Understanding the basic principles of power is critical in order to control or manipulate power.
Answer: True

Pages: 344
5. We communicate power verbally but not nonverbally.
Answer: False

Pages: 343
6. Interpersonal power is what enables one person to control others' behaviors.
Answer: True

Pages: 349
7. If you let others play power games without any form of retaliation, you communicate that you have enough power that you do not need to play.
Answer: False

Pages: 359
8. Nonassertive people often ask permission from others to do what they already have a perfect right to do.
Answer: True

Pages: 360
9. Assertive people are contentious.
Answer: True

Pages: 360
10. Assertive people are always assertive.
Answer: False

Short Answer

Write the word or phrase that best completes each statement or answers the question.

Pages: 342
1. In order to increase self-esteem, engage in _____.
   Answer: self-affirmation

Pages: 342
2. The way we _____ to ourselves about ourselves will influence what we _____ of ourselves.
   Answer: talk, think

Pages: 343
3. _____ permeates all our interpersonal relationships.
   Answer: power

Pages: 344
4. Some people are more _____ than others.
   Answer: powerful

Pages: 348
5. Expressions that convey a lack of competence are called _____.
   Answer: disqualifiers

Pages: 356
6. Saying that you will feel better if you comply is an example of

   _____.
   Answer: positive self-feelings

Pages: 347
7. No interpersonal relationship exists without a _____.
   Answer: power dimension

Pages: 350
8. In the power play, _____, someone does something for you and then demands something in return.
   Answer: you owe me

9. In the power play, _____, the individual refuses to acknowledge your request.
   Answer: nobody upstairs

10. Assertive behavior allows a person to act in his or her own _____ without denying the
    _____ of others.
    Answer: best interests, rights

Essay

Write your answer in the space provided or on a separate sheet of paper.

1. Explain to a friend six different ways to increase their self-esteem.
   Answer: attack self-destructive beliefs, seek out nourishing people, work on projects
            that will result in success, engage in self-affirmation, you do not have to
            succeed in everything you do, and you do not need to be loved by everyone

2. Explain the principles of power with a brief example of each one.
   Answer: some people are more powerful than others, all interpersonal messages have a
            power dimension, all interpersonal encounters involve power, power follows the
            principle of least interest

3. Explain the principles for increasing assertiveness.
   Answer: analyze the assertive behavior of others, rehearse assertive behavior, do it

Chapter 1: Interpersonal Communication
1-1: Purposes
1-2: Definition
1-3: Dyads
1-4: Elements
1-5: Decoding
1-6: Competence
1-7: Noise
1-8: Context
1-9: Ethics
1-10: Principles
1-11: Content/Relationship
1-12: Irreversible
1-13: Critical Thinking
1-14: STEP

Chapter 2: The Self
2-1: Self-Concept
2-2: Johari Window
2-3: Self-Awareness
2-4: Factors
2-5: Gender
2-6: Rewards
2-7: Dangers
2-8: Guidelines for Making Self-Disclosures
2-9: Guidelines for Responding
2-10: Apprehension
2-11: Confidence

Chapter 3: Perception in Interpersonal Communication
3-1: Definition
3-2: Elephant

6-8:   Touch
6-9:   Voice
6-10: Paralinguistics
6-11: Silence
6-12: Time Communication

Chapter 7:   Emotional Messages
7-1:   Components
7-2:   Theories
7-3:   Emotions
7-4:   Feelings
7-5:   Obstacles
7-6:   Guidelines
7-7:   Describe Feelings
7-8:   Identify Reasons
7-9:   I-Messages
7-10: Grief

Chapter 8:   Conversation Messages
8-1:   Model
8-2:   Feedforward
8-3:   Disclaimers
8-4:   Initiating
8-5:   Maintain
8-6:   Excuses
8-7:   Closing
8-8:   Metaskills
8-9:   Effectiveness
8-10: Immediacy

Chapter 9:   Interpersonal Communication and Culture
9-1:   Importance
9-2:   Culture
9-3:   Forms
9-4:   Ethnocentrism
9-5:   Ignore
9-6:   Differences
9-7:   Meaning
9-8:   Violate
9-9:   Evaluate
9-10: Barriers

Chapter 10: Interpersonal Communication and Relationships

10-1: Reasons
10-2: Friends
10-3: Stage Talk
10-4: Love
10-5: Repair
10-6: Attraction
10-7: Marry
10-8: Social Penetration
10-9: Social Exchange
10-10: Equity

Chapter 11: Interpersonal Communication and Conflict

11-1: Conflict
11-2: Negative
11-3: Positives
11-4: Model
11-5: Hats
11-6: Strategies
11-7: Aggressiveness
11-8: Argumentativeness
11-9: Before Conflict
11-10: After Conflict

Chapter 12: Interpersonal Communication and Power

12-1: Self-Esteem
12-2: Increasing Self-Esteem
12-3: Power
12-4: Principles
12-5: Communicate
12-6: Power Plays
12-7: Compliance
12-8: Resisting
12-9: Assertiveness
12-10: Increasing Assertiveness

Five Purposes of Interpersonal Communication

1. to learn   4. to play

2. to relate   5. to help

3. to influence

Interpersonal Communication

Interpersonal communication is

communication that takes place between

two persons who have a relationship

between them.

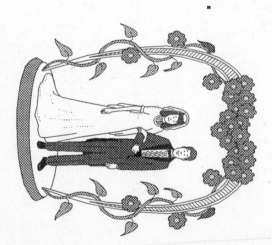

Dyads   Dyads

Two's company; three's a crowd.

Nine-tenths of the people were created so you would want to be with the other tenth.

For this reason a man shall leave his father and mother, and be made one with his wife; and the two shall become one flesh.

Elements of
Interpersonal Communication

Source-Receiver   Noise

Messages   Context

Feedback   Competence

Feedforward   Ethics

Channel

Your task, should you choose to accept it, is to find the code for each of the   messages below. Then, fill in the blanks.

Decode a Message

1.   1, 3, 5, ___

2.   2, ___, 10, 14, 18

3.   13, 8, 12, ___, 11, 10

4.   64, 32, 48, 24, ___, 18

5.   4, 9, 16, ___, 36

6.   4, 16, ___, 65536

7.   8, 11, 15, ___, 4, 14, 9, ___, 7, 6, 10, ___, 3, 12, 2

Interpersonal Competence

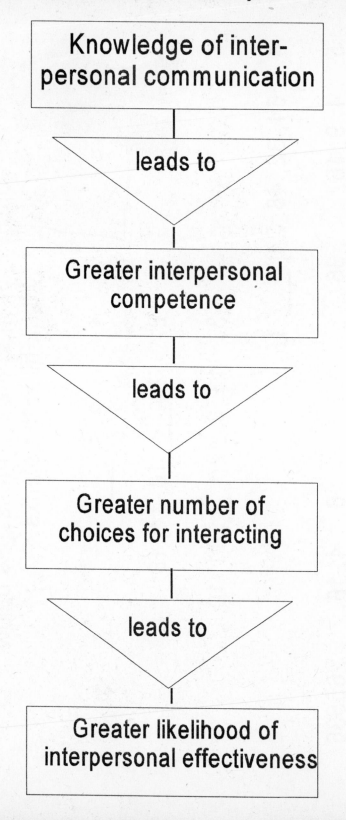

Knowledge of inter-
personal communication

leads to

Greater interpersonal
competence

leads to

Greater number of
choices for interacting

leads to

Greater likelihood of
interpersonal effectiveness

NOISE!

1. Physical

2. Psychological

3. Semantic

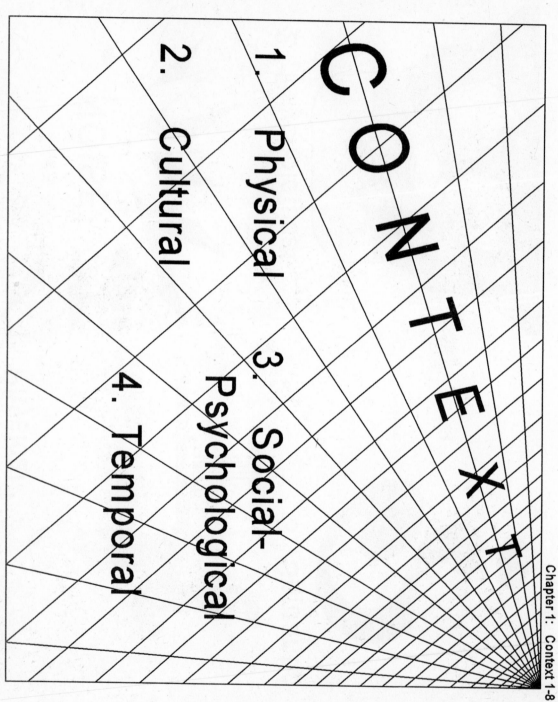

CONTEXT

1. Physical
2. Cultural
3. Social-Psychological
4. Temporal

Would you:

E xaggerate your virtues to get a job?

T ell the truth if it causes hurt feelings?

H old threats or promises over someone?

I gnore someone else's cheating?

C onceal your emotions from your partner?

S wear you'll keep a secret -- and then tell?

1. Communication is transactional.

2. Communication involves content and relationship messages.

3. Communication is inevitable.

4. Communication is irreversible and unrepeatable.

Principles of Interpersonal Communication

Relationship:

COMMUNICATION

Content:

Try NOT to think of a pink rhinoceros!

Critical Thinking

Ask questions

Identify assumptions

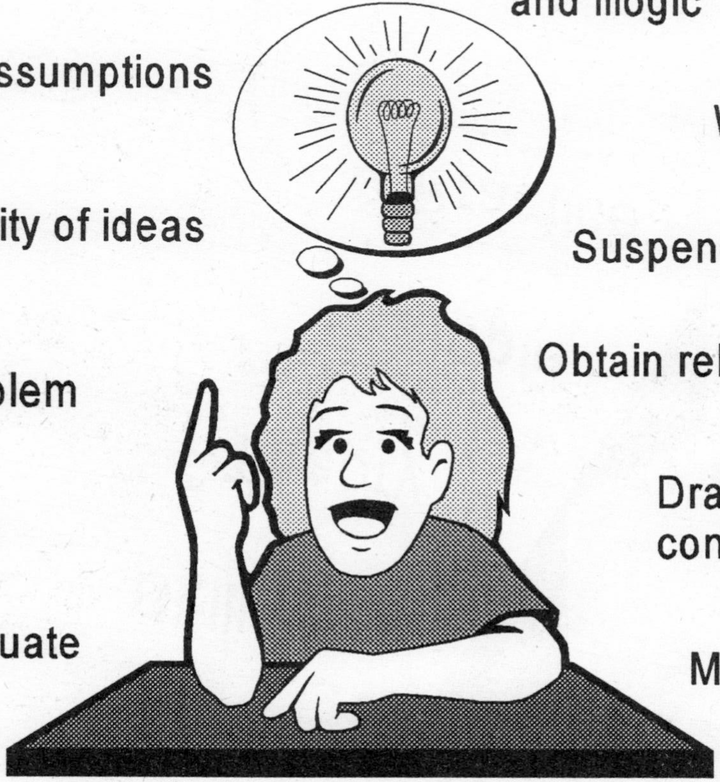

Evaluate quality of ideas

Define problem

Organize

Esplore and evaluate strategies

Distinguish between logic and illogic

Weigh truth

Suspend judgment

Obtain relevant information

Draw and evaluate conclusions

Make connections

STEP

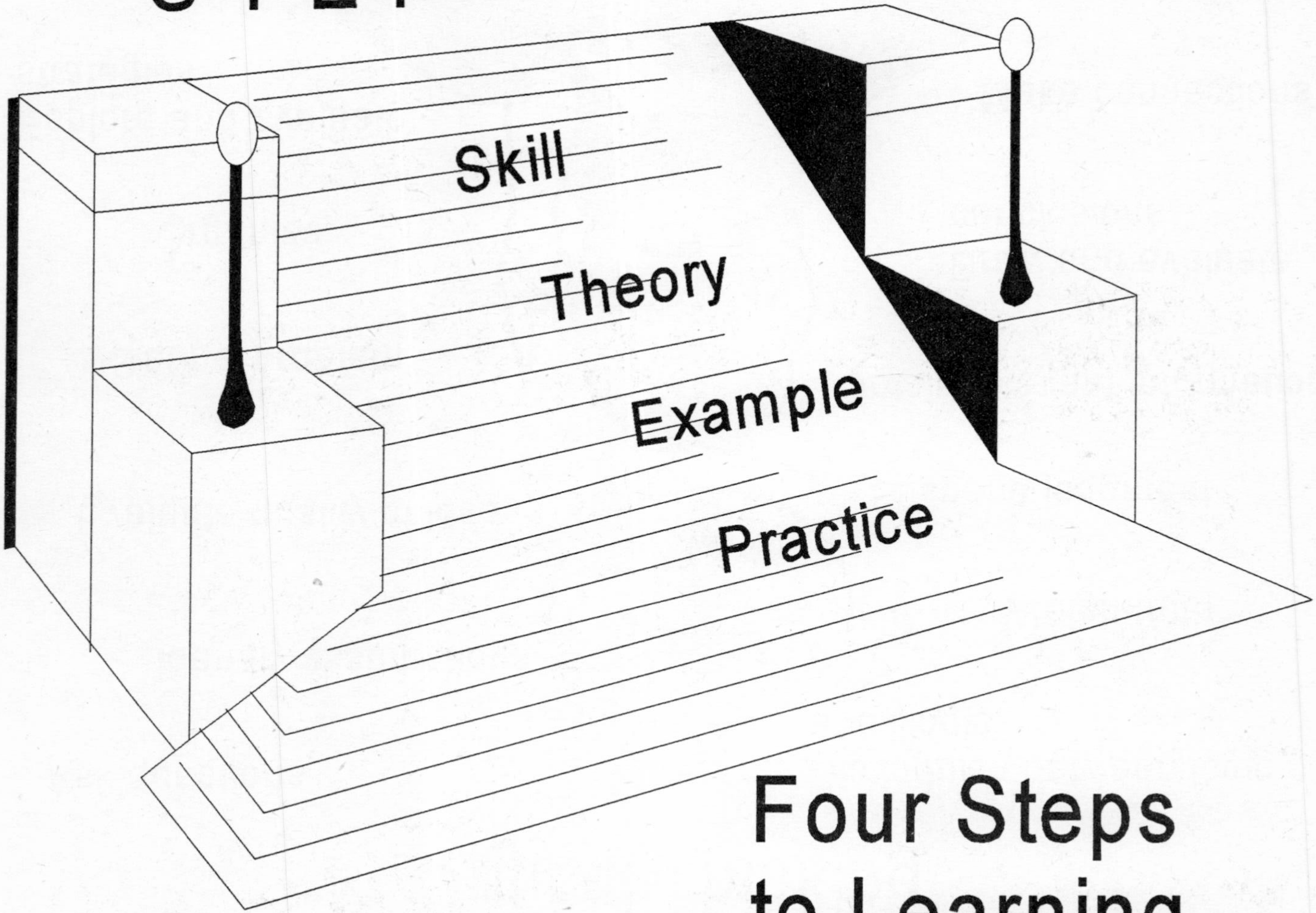

Skill

Theory

Example

Practice

Four Steps
to Learning

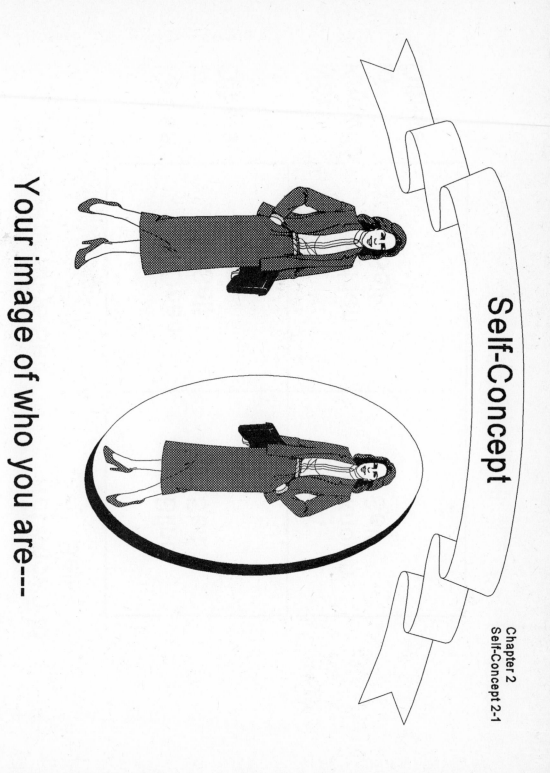

Your image of who you are---

Self-Concept

Johari Window

	Known to Self	Not Known to Self
Known to Others	Open Self	Blind Self
Not Known to Others	Hidden Self	Unknown Self

Increasing Self-Awareness:
Why and How

Why?

to identify strengths
and weaknesses

to direct energy to
correct weaknesses

to improve interpersonal
communication

to gain greater control
over yourself

How?

Listen to others

Increase your open self

Seek information about
yourself

Factors Influencing Self-Disclosure

Self-disclosure occurs more readily with:

small groups

people we like

competent people

extroverted people

others also disclosing

some topics

the U.S. culture

feminine sex roles

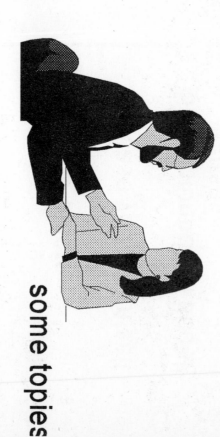

Self-Disclosure:
Gender Differences

Reasons women don't self-disclose:

1. Information may be used against me

2. Sign of emotional disturbance

3. Might hurt a relationship

Reasons men don't self-disclose:

1. Might make me appear inconsistent

2. Might lose control over the other person

3. Might threaten relationships other than close ones

Rewards

As a result of your self-disclosure, you hereby receive:

Greater self-knowledge

Increased communication effectiveness

Better physiological health

DANGER!!!

"Uncensored candor is a bad idea."

Arthur Bochner

Risks:

to one's job

to professional
advancement

to social and
family life

Guidelines for Making Self-Disclosures

1. What is your motivation for self-disclosing?

2. Is this self-disclosure appropriate?

3. Is the other person also disclosing?

4. Will this self-disclosure impose burdens?

Guidelines for Responding to Self-Disclosures

1. Practice effective and active listening.

2. Support the discloser.

3. Keep the disclosures confidential.

Communication Apprehension

"Communication apprehension is probably the most common handicap suffered by people in contemporary American society."

McCroskey & Wheeless, 1976

Managing Apprehension

Acquire communication skills and experience

Focus on success

Reduce unpredictability

Put apprehension in perspective

You can do it!

Interpersonal Perception

The way we:

1. Sense

2. Organize

3. Interpret-Evaluate

information about people

The Parable of the
Six Blind Men of Indostan

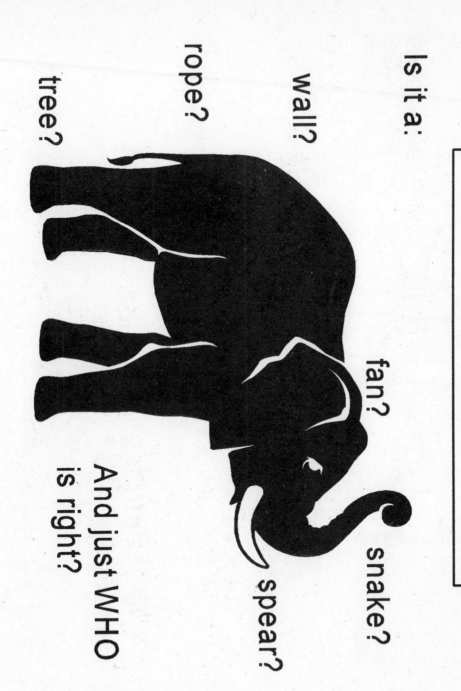

Is it a:

wall?

rope?

tree?

fan?

snake?

spear?

And just WHO
is right?

How do you react to each of the following images?

Is your reaction positive or negative?

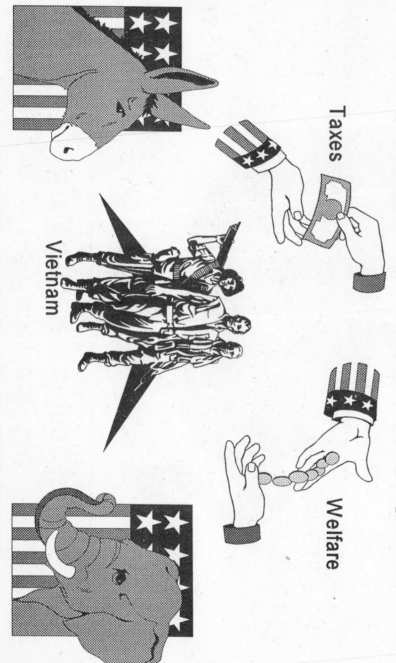

Taxes

Vietnam

Welfare

Four Psychological Processes

1. First impressions

2. Theories in our heads

3. Self-Fulfilling Prophecies

4. Stereotypes

5. Attributions

You never have

a second chance

to make a

first impression.

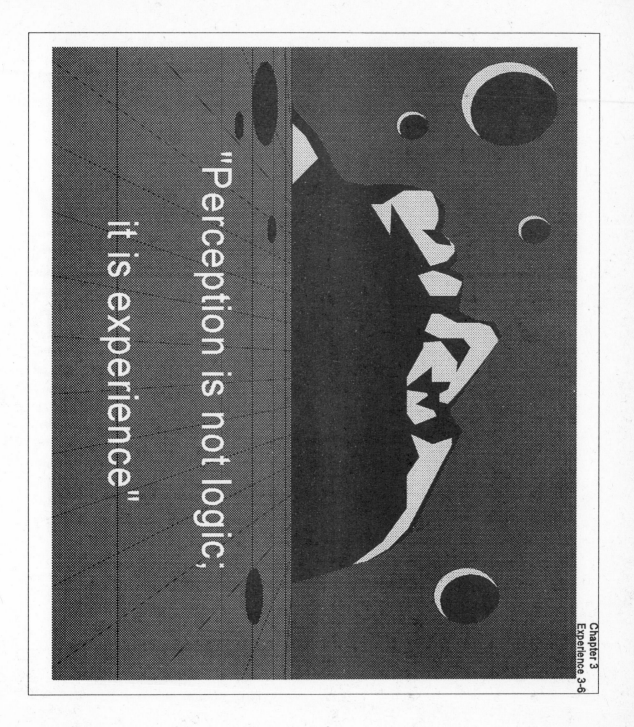

"Perception is not logic; it is experience"

Stereotypes

Blondes

Professors

Jocks

Computer Nerds

People with glasses

Gays and Lesbians

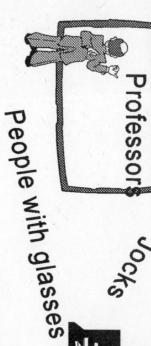

Jews

Women Drivers

Blacks

Artists

Hispanics

Perception Checking:

1. Describe what you think is happening.
2. Ask the other person for confirmation.

Barriers to Effective Perception

First Impressions

Implicit Theories

Prophecies

Stereotypes

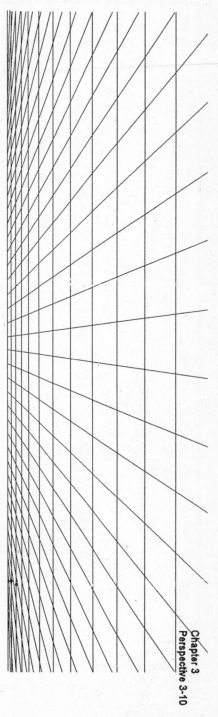
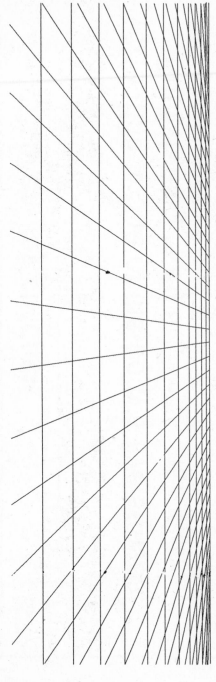

Taking the perspective of another
person is not easy, BUT
it is the MOST important thing you
can do to achieve mutual understanding.

"Listen, my children. . . . "

"Hearing is one of the body's five senses.
But listening is an art."

Frank Tyger

"We have been given two ears and but a
single mouth in order that we may hear
more and talk less."

Zeno of Citium

"Hear twice before you speak once."

Scottish saying

Why Do We Listen?

To learn

To play

To help

To relate

To influence

The Five Processes
of Listening

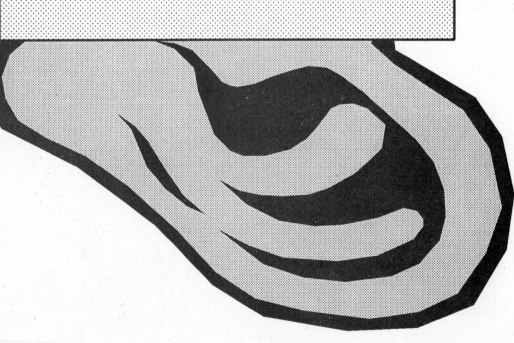

Receiving

Understanding

Remembering

Evaluating

Responding

Memory Test

Bed   Dream   Comfort

Rest   Wake   Sound

Awake   Night   Slumber

Tired   Eat   Snore

Dimensions of Listening

Participatory	Passive
Empathic	Objective
Nonjudgmental	Critical
Surface	Depth

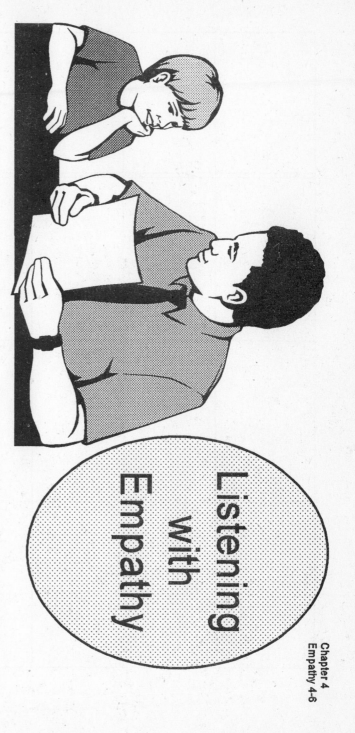

Listening from the point of view of the speaker -- not your own

Responding to the speaker's needs -- not your own

Listening
with
Empathy

Listening for Message Distortions

Speaker	Leveling	Sharpening	Assimilation

"Actions speak louder than words."

Active Listening

The process of understanding the whole message: verbal and nonverbal, content and feelings

Techniques of Active Listening

Paraphrase the speaker's thoughts.

Express understanding of the speaker's feelings.

Ask questions.

Meaning in Interpersonal Communication

Meanings are denotative . . . and connotative.

"Democratic"

"Freedom"

Meanings are in people . . . . not in words.

Beware of High-Order Abstractions

T.V. Shows   Bucket   Evil   Freedom

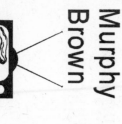

Murphy Brown

Colonel Sanders

Rock Music

Driver's License

Barrier 1: Polarization

" ...looking at the world in terms of opposites; describing it in extremes."

RIGHT WRONG

- -

To Avoid: Use middle terms:

" ...alternatives between the extremes."

NEUTRAL

Barrier 2: Intensional Orientation

" ...to view people, objects, and events in the way they are labeled."

"He's all wet--"

- - - - - - - - - -

To avoid: Extensionalize

Here he is: the dry look -- and a different impression

Barrier 3: Fact-Inference Confusion

"...confusing statements about what you observe and those about what you have not observed."

CARRY A BRIEFCASE   CARRY A GRUDGE

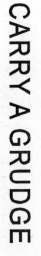

To Avoid: Distinguish Facts from Inferences

Use tentative language:

"As far as I know,"   "As I see it,"   "It may be,"
   "It seems to me," "I think"

Barrier 4: Static Evaluation

"…acting as if everything were not in a state of constant change."

Person 1   =   Person 1

To Avoid: Focus on change; Date your statements

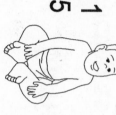

≠

Person 1
2 / 7 / 95

Person 1
10/ 15 / 05

Barrier 5: Allness

"Thinking and acting as if you know everything"

The Parable of the
Six Blind Men of Indostan

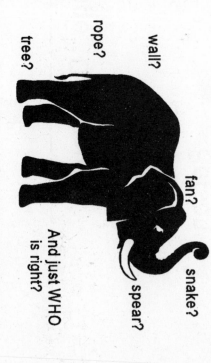

wall?

rope?

tree?

fan?

snake?

spear?

And just WHO
is right?

To Avoid: Recognize there is more to know
about every topic

End your statements with "ETC."

Be open to additional information.

Barrier 6: Indiscrimination

" ...focus on classes of
individuals or events,
and fail to see each
as unique."

"Politician."

To Avoid: Index your terms

Politician
1

Politician
2

Disconfirmation

Language Racism - used by members of one
culture to disparage members
of other cultures

Language Sexism   - Generic "man"
Generic "he" and "his"
Sex role stereotyping

Language Heterosexism
- used to disparage gay
men and lesbians

What do these headlines _____ mean?

Jerk Injures Neck, Wins Award

St. Louis Post-Dispatch

Doctor Testifies in Horse Suit

Waterbury (Conn.) Republican

Sex education delayed, teachers request training

Saint Croix Courier

U's food service feeds thousands, **grosses millions**

The Minnesota Daily

Nonverbal Communication

Messages communicated without words:

Forms of Nonverbal Communication

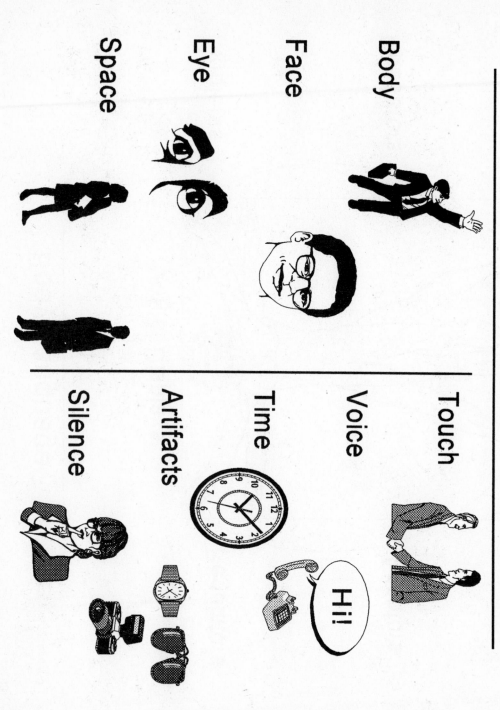

Body

Face

Eye

Space

Touch

Voice

Time

Artifacts

Silence

Hi!

Body Language

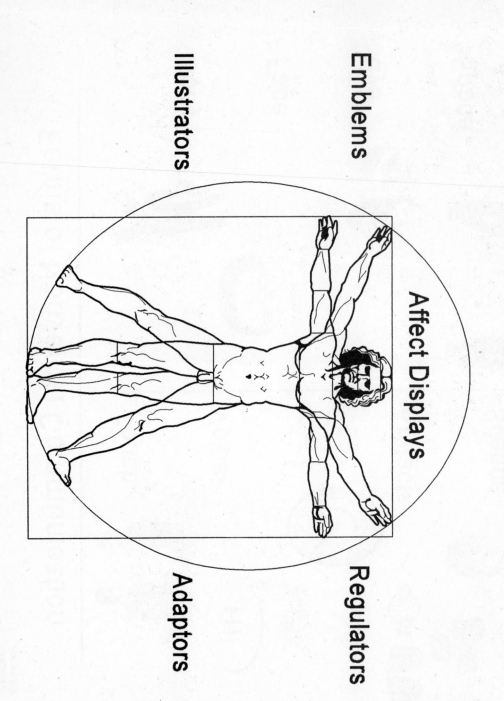

Illustrators

Emblems

Affect Displays

Regulators

Adaptors

Faces:

Eye Communication

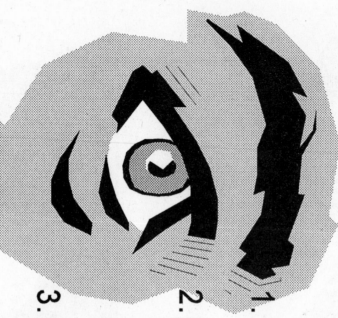

PURPOSES:

1. Give and get feedback

2. Inform that the channel of communication is open

3. Signal the nature of the relationship

4. Establish dominance

Spatial Distances

Intimate (0 - 18 inches)

Personal (1 1/2 - 4 feet)

Social (4 - 12 feet)

Public (12 - 25 feet)

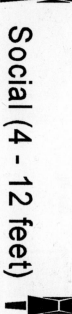

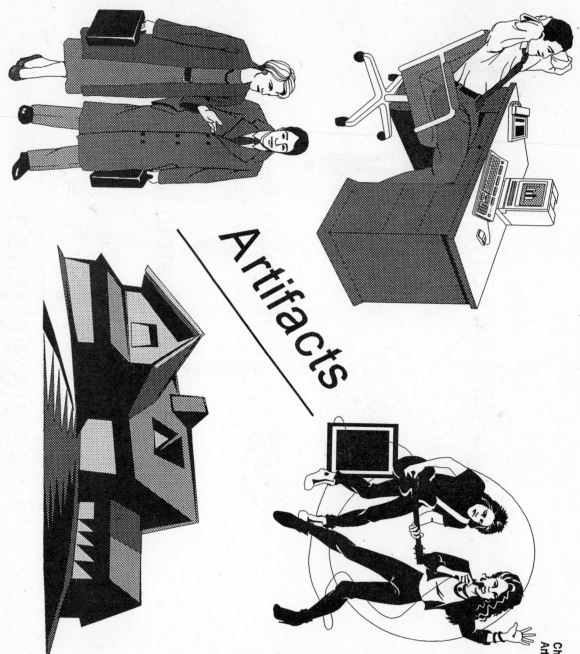

Artifacts

Meanings of Touch

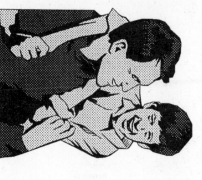

Playfulness

Positive Emotion

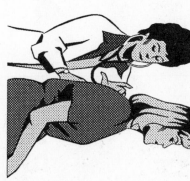

Task-Related

Ritual

Control

Your voice ...

Rate

Pitch

Rhythm

Volume

Paralinguistics

I would not say

you lost the fight.

Silence:

- Allows time to think

- Can be used to hurt

- Might indicate anxiety

- May prevent certain messages

- Can communicate emotions

- Says, "I have nothing to say."

Time Communication

Cultural Time:

Formal

Informal

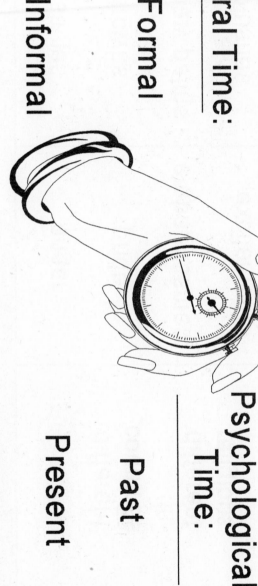

Psychological Time:

Past

Present

Future

Three Components of Emotions

Body	Mind	Culture
smiles	anger	different countries
frowns	pride	different religions
sweaty palms	embarrassment	different sex roles
blushes	excitement	
kisses	delight	
shaky knees	hurt	
vocal hesitations	satisfaction	

Theories of Emotions

1. Am I scared because I see the bear?

   Commonsense Theory

2. Am I scared because my knees are shaking, my heart is pounding, and I can hardly breathe?

   James-Lange Theory

3. Am I scared because I have decided that shaky knees, pounding hearts, and inability to breathe are logical physical responses to a threat?

   Cognitive-Labeling Theory

Emotions

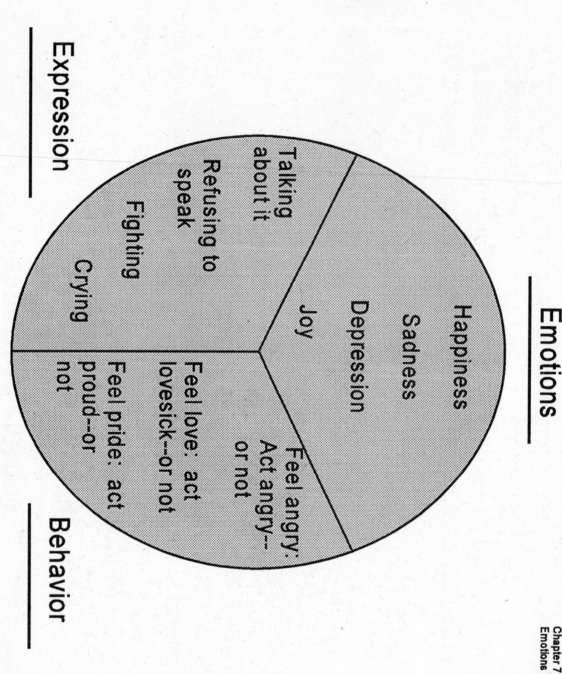

Expression

Talking about it

Refusing to speak

Fighting

Crying

Behavior

Joy

Depression

Sadness

Happiness

Feel angry: Act angry—or not

Feel love: act lovesick—or not

Feel pride: act proud—or not

"If you let your mind control your heart, you lose touch with the feelings that give life meaning."

"The heart has its reasons which reason knows nothing of."

Blaise Pascal

Obstacles in Communicating Emotions

Social Rules: Cowboy Syndrome

Inadequate Interpersonal Skills

Fear of Exposing Weakness

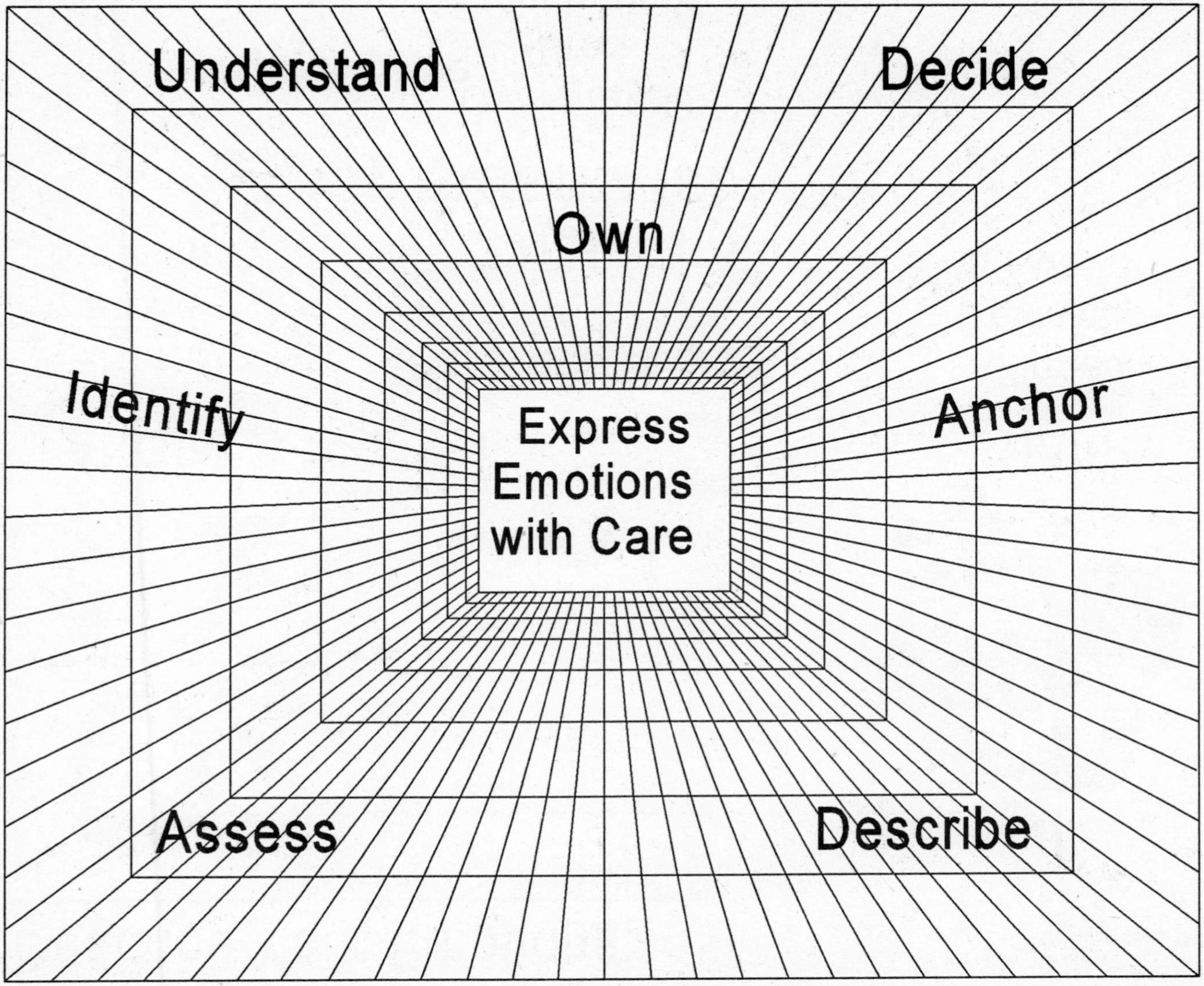

Identify

Assess

Understand

Express
Emotions
with Care

Own

Describe

Anchor

Decide

Describe Your Emotions:

ANGRY

Hurt
Afraid
Surprised

FRUSTRATED

Overworked
Tired
Incompetent

HAPPY

Affirmed
Optimistic
In Control

Identify the Reasons for Your Feelings

WHY?

To understand:

HOW and WHY
you feel as you do

To discover:

WHAT TO DO
to get rid of
negative feelings

I own my own feelings.

YOU cannot MAKE me

feel anything!

Communicating with the Grief-Stricken

1. Confirm the person and their feelings.

2. Give permission to grieve.

3. Don't force the bright side.

4. Encourage expression of feelings.

5. Empathize.

6. Be sensitive to leave-taking cues.

The Conversational Process

1. Opening

"Hi! What's going on?"

2. Feedforward

"I hate to bother you, but.."

3. Business

"I've just found a new way to import a file."

4. Feedback

"So you may want to try it."

5. Closing

"Gotta go…"

Feedforward

"Feedforward tells the listener something about the message to come."

1. It may open communication.

2. It may preview future messages.

3. It may altercast, or place the receiver in a specific role.

4. It may offer a disclaimer.

Before we begin---
a set of disclaimers:

Hedging — Disclaim the importance of the message to the speaker

Credentialing — Speaker knows message will not be liked but will say it anyway

Sin License — Speaker is going to violate a rule

Cognitive Disclaimer — Speaker anticipates listener will doubt his/her good sense

Appeal for judgment to be suspended — Speaker asks listener to delay making judgment

Initiating a Conversation:

Make references to:

SELF

OTHERS

RELATIONSHIP

CONTEXT

1. Be positive.

2. Disclose appropriately.

BOTH can regulate the conversation.

Speaker Cues	Listener Cues
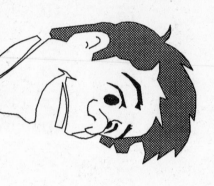	

Turn-maintaining cues

Turn-yielding cues

Turn-requesting cues

Turn-denying cues

Backchanneling cues

Sometimes you get in a conversational can of worms!

Excuses might help:

TRY:

"I didn't do it!"

"It wasn't so bad."

or

"Yes, but..."

Closing a conversation:

1. Reflect back on the conversation.

2. State your desire to end the conversation.

3. Refer to future interaction.

4. Ask for closure.

5. State that you enjoyed the interaction.

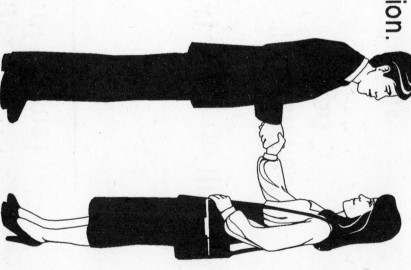

Communication Metaskills

1. Mindfulness

2. F l e x i b i l i t y

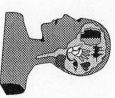

3. Cultural Sensitivity

4. Metacommunicational Ability

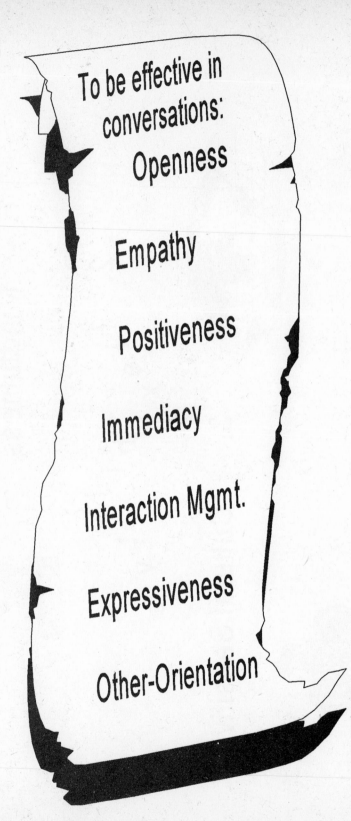

IMMEDIACY

Verbal:

1. Focus on the other's remarks. Let the speaker know you understood.

2. Reinforce, reward, or compliment the other person.

Nonverbal:

1. Maintain eye contact; smile and express interest.

2. Maintain physical closeness; maintain open and direct body posture.

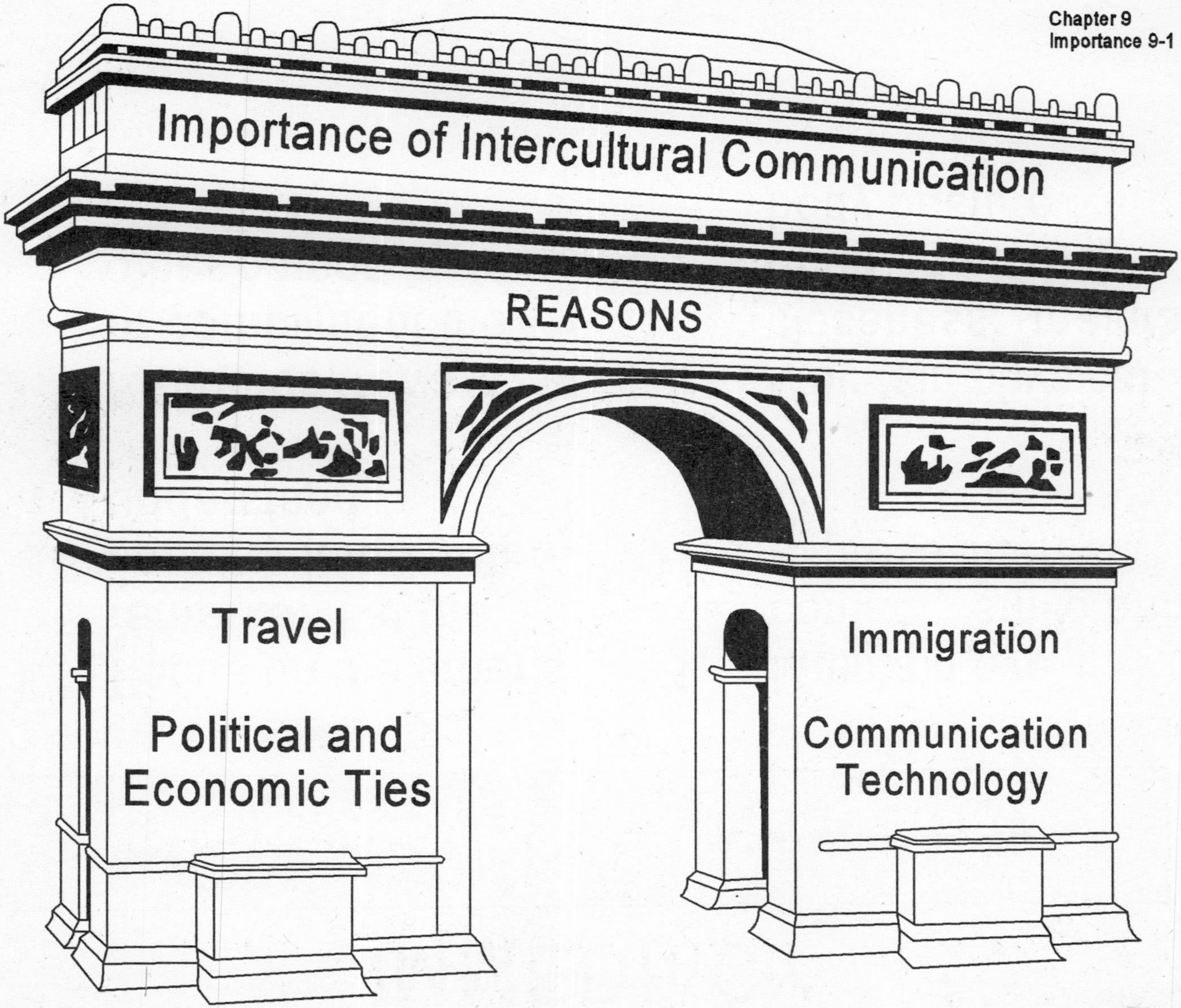

Importance of Intercultural Communication

REASONS

Political and Economic Ties

Travel

Communication Technology

Immigration

Culture

...the relatively specialized lifestyle
of a group of people:

values
beliefs
artifacts
behavior
communication
language
ways of thinking
art
laws
religion

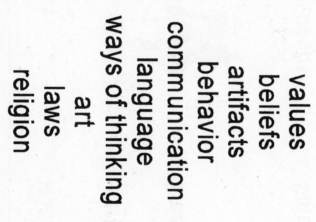

Forms of Intercultural Communication

Communication between:

Cultures   Nations

Races   Small Cultures

Ethnic Groups   Small Groups

Religions   Sexes

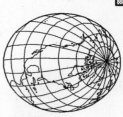

Ethnocentrism

We all have tendency to see others and their behaviors through our own cultural filters...

...and evaluate our culture's values, beliefs, and behaviors as more positive, superior, logical, and natural than those of other cultures.

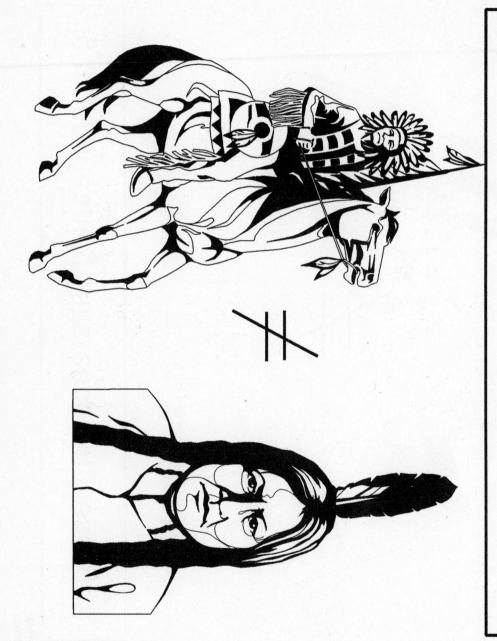

Ignoring Differences Within Other Groups

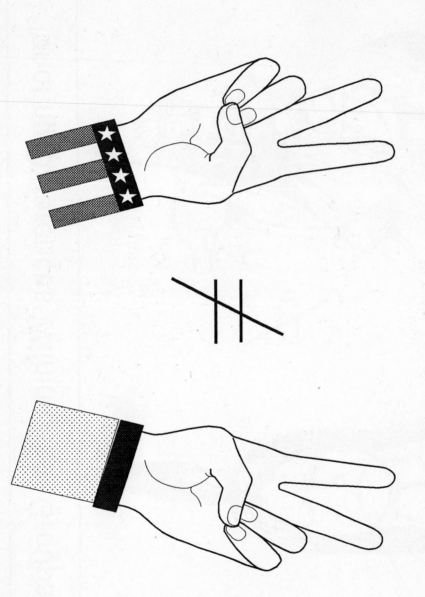

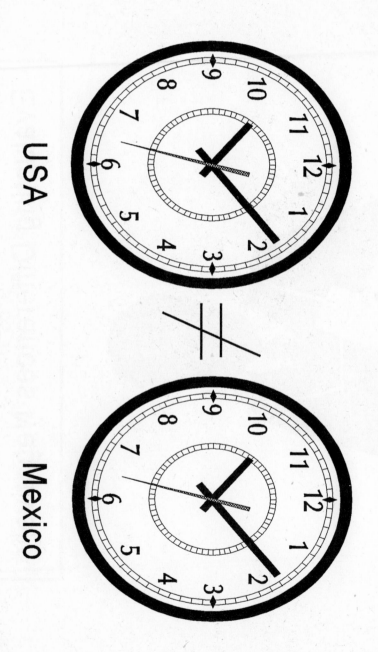

Violating Cultural Rules and Customs

USA

Mexico

Evaluating Differences Negatively

Try not to judge cultural differences; see them as different but equal.

Avoid the Common Intercultural Barriers

1. Recognize differences between yourself and the other person.

2. Recognize differences exist within any group.

3. Remember meaning is in the person, not in words or gestures.

4. Be aware of cultural rules, and be sensitive.

5. Avoid negative evaluation of cultural differences.

Reasons for Relationships

1. Lessen loneliness

2. Stimulate ideas

3. Learn about yourself

4. Enhance self-esteem

5. Maximize physical, mental, & social pleasures

6. Minimize pain

Friendship

"Love demands infinitely less than friendship."

George Jean Nathan

"True friendship is like sound health:
the value of it is seldom known
until it be lost."

Charles Caleb Colton

"We cherish our friends not for their
ability to amuse us, but for ours
to amuse them."

Evelyn Waugh

6 Stages in Relationships

CONTACT
Hello, how are you?
May I join you?
Haven't we met before?

INVOLVEMENT
I'd like to know you better.
Is your mother feeling ill?
I'm voting for her, too.

INTIMACY
We have a lot in common.
I care about you.
Will you marry me?

DETERIORATION
I feel stifled.
We aren't Siamese twins.
You never talk to me now.

REPAIR
I am concerned about us.
I'm willing to try; are you?
What do you say is wrong?

DISSOLUTION
It's all over.
I gave it everything I had.
I'm moving out tonight.

Love

Eros

Ludus

Storge

Pragma

Mania

Agape

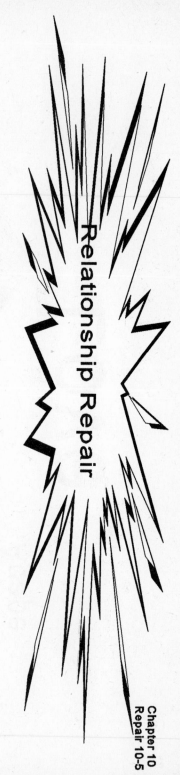

Relationship Repair

General Relationship Repair Strategies

1. Recognize the problem

2. Engage in productive conflict resolution

3. Pose possible solutions

4. Affirm each other

5. Integrate solutions into normal behavior

6. Risk

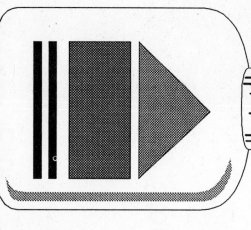

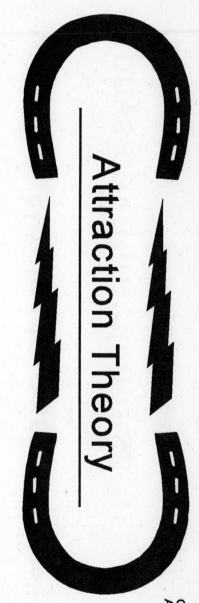

Attraction Theory

Attractiveness
(Physical and Personality)

Similarity

Proximity

Reinforcement

Similarity

Similarity

We date and mate with people

who are similar to ourselves

in physical attractiveness.

Social Penetration

Depth

From
Superficial
to
Intense

Breadth

Range of Topics

Social Exchange Theory

Profits = Rewards - Costs

Equity Theory

We develop and maintain relationships in which the ratio of our rewards compared to costs is approximately equal to our partner's.

Conflict!

Relationship Conflict:

When people have opposing goals and interfere with each other's attainment of those goals

The Negatives of Conflict

Increased negative regard for the opponent

Depletion of energy

Isolation from others

Increased costs; decreased rewards

The Positives of Conflict

Values of interpersonal conflict:

 Forces the examination of a problem

 Moves toward potential solutions

 Enables individuals to state desires -- and get them

 Prevents hostilities from festering

 Increases understanding and meeting each other's needs

 Says relationship is worth the effort

A Conflict Model

Define conflict

Remember content and relationship
Use specific terms
See the other's point of view
Check perception -- and definitions

Define possible solutions

Look for win-win solutions
Weigh costs and rewards
Seek solutions where rewards are shared

Test solution

Test mentally: how does it feel today?
                   how will it feel tomorrow?
Test in actual operation: does it work?

Evaluate solution

Did it resolve the conflict?
Is the situation better?
Is it worth it? Are rewards and costs even? Use critical thinking hats.

Accept or Reject

Accept solution: put it into operation

Reject solution: test another solution
                  re-define the conflict

Critical Thinking Hats

Fact Hat

Feeling Hat

Negative
Argument Hat

Control of Thinking
Hat

Creative
New Idea Hat

Positive
Benefits Hat

Conflict Management Strategies

Productive	Destructive
Fight Actively	Avoidance
Talk	Force
Supportiveness	Defensiveness
Empathy	Blame
Open Expression	Silencers
Present Focus	Gunnysack
Above the Belt	Below the Belt
Argumentativeness	Aggressiveness

Verbal Aggressiveness

- Inflicts psychological pain

- Attacks self-concept

- Disconfirms

- Discredits one's view of self

BEFORE CONFLICT:

Fight in private.
Be ready to fight.
Know what you're fighting about.
Define the problem.
Fight about problems that can
be solved.

AFTER CONFLICT

Learn from the conflict.

Keep the conflict in perspective.

Attack your negative feelings.

Increase the exchange of rewards.

Self-Esteem

If you think like
a winner ---

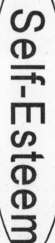

You are likely to
BE a winner!

If you think you are
going to bomb ---

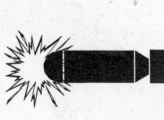

You probably will!

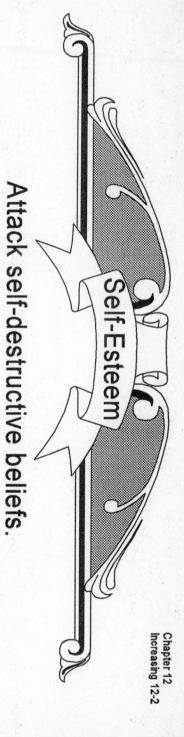

Self-Esteem

Attack self-destructive beliefs.

Seek out nourishing people.

Work on projects that will be successful.

You do not need to succeed in everything
or be loved by everyone.

Engage in self-affirmation.

POWER!

Power allows control over the behaviors of others.

Principles of Power

Some people are more powerful than others.

All interpersonal messages have a power dimension.

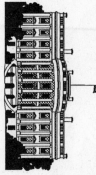

All interpersonal encounters involve power.

Power follows the principle of least interest.

More Powerful Speech

Powerful:

This is a great book.

Neutral:

I like this book.

Powerless:

This, um, is a book I think, er, that you might kind of like, don't you think?

Power Plays

Power Plays	Cooperative Response
1. Nobody upstairs	1. Express your feelings.
2. You owe me	2. Describe the behavior to which you object.
3. Metaphor	3. State a cooperative response.
4. Yougottobekidding	
5. Thought stoppers	

Compliance-Gaining Strategies

Definition: tactics that influence others to do what you want them to do.

"The only prize much cared for by the powerful is power. The prize of the general is not a bigger tent, but command."

Oliver Wendell Holmes, Jr.

Compliance-Resisting Strategies

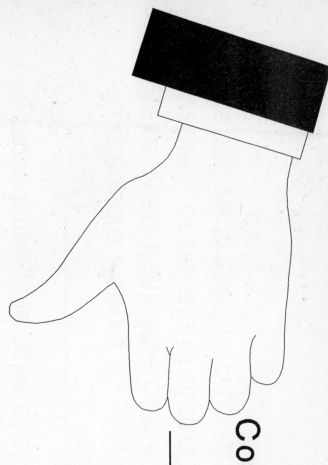

Identity
management:
* positive
* negative

Non-negotiation
Negotiation
Justification

Nonassertive People:
are timid, reserved, and unable to assert their rights

Assertive People:
act in their own best interests, stand up for themselves, express honest feelings, and exercise their rights without denying the rights of others

Aggressive People:
take over; think little of the opinions, values, or beliefs of others; and are sensitive to the criticism of others

Analyze the
assertive behavior
of others.

Rehearse assertive
behaviors.

Do it!!